D1588175

The Tudors
A Very Peculiar History™

With even more executions!

'The most dangerous and cruel man
in the world.'

Henry VIII described by the
French ambassador, Castillon

For my mother – who loves a
costume drama with a high body count!
JP

Editor: Stephen Haynes
Additional artwork: Mark Bergin, John James,
David Salariya, Shirley Willis, Gerald Wood

Published in Great Britain in MMXI by
Book House, an imprint of
The Salariya Book Company Ltd
25 Marlborough Place, Brighton BN1 1UB
www.salariya.com
www.book-house.co.uk

HB ISBN-13: 978-1-907184-58-1

1 3 5 7 9 8 6 4 2
A CIP catalogue record for this book is available
from the British Library.
Printed and bound in Dubai.
Printed on paper from sustainable sources.

Visit our website at **www.book-house.co.uk**
or go to **www.salariya.com**
for **free** electronic versions of:
You Wouldn't Want to be an Egyptian Mummy!
You Wouldn't Want to be a Roman Gladiator!
You Wouldn't Want to be a Polar Explorer!
You Wouldn't Want to sail on a 19th-Century
Whaling Ship!

The Tudors
A Very Peculiar History™

With even more executions!

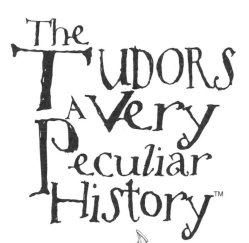

Jim Pipe

Created and designed by
David Salariya

Illustrated by
David Antram

'You have sent me
a Flanders mare!'

Henry VIII, angry that Anne of
Cleves was less attractive than her
portrait suggested

'Mary, Mary, quite contrary,
How does your garden grow?
With silver bells
and cockleshells
And pretty maids all in a row.'

This nursery rhyme may refer to
Mary I's attempts to make
England Catholic again

'I know I have the body
of a weak and feeble woman,
but I have the heart and
stomach of a king, and of a king
of England too.'

Elizabeth I to her army at Tilbury
in 1588

Contents

Some right royal sayings

'We are, by the sufferance of God, King of England; and the Kings of England in times past never had any superior but God.'

Henry VIII to Cardinal Wolsey, 1515

'I will make you shorter by a head.'

Elizabeth I's retort to anyone who was taller than her and disagreed with her.

'I have already joined myself in marriage to a husband, namely the kingdom of England. Do not blame me for the miserable lack of children, for every one of you are children of mine.'

Elizabeth's answer to critics who said she should marry and raise a family.

'Let every man have his doctor. This is mine.'

Said by Henry VIII as he toasted the Dean of Westminster with a glass of wine, 1513

'With your head and my purse I could do anything.'

Elizabeth I praises her minister William Cecil

'Pastime with good company
I love, and shall until I die.
Grouch who list,[1] but none deny;
So God be pleased, thus live will I.
   To my pastance,[2]
   Hunt, sing and dance,
   My heart is set;
   All goodly sport
   For my comfort –
   Who shall me let?'[3]

First verse of a song attributed to Henry VIII

'The most obstinate woman that ever was.'

*Thomas Cromwell writing about Mary I,
June 1536*

'I'm reasonably sorry.'

*Philip II of Spain on hearing that his wife
Mary I had died.*

'When anyone speaks of her beauty, she says she
was never beautiful. Nevertheless, she speaks of
her beauty as often as she can.'

*André Hurault, Sieur de Maisse, French
ambassador to Elizabeth's court, 1597*

*1. Grouch who list: Let people complain if they want to.
2. pastance: pleasure.   3. let: prevent.*

Putting the Tudors on the map

Pinkie Cleugh
Flodden
Edinburgh
York
Pontefract
Lincoln
Chester
Ludlow
Beaumaris
Mortimer's Cross
Carmarthen
Raglan
Pembroke
London

Ipswich
Beaulieu (Essex)
Tilbury
Leeds Castle
Dover
Margate
Ightham Mote
Knole
Eltham Palace
Blackheath
Hever
Greenwich
Barnet
Hunsdon
Hatfield House
Richmond
Windsor
Ewelme
Hampton Court
Farnham Palace
Nonsuch
Isle of Wight
Portsmouth
Longleat
Woodstock
Kenilworth
Bosworth Field
Fotheringhay
Leicester
Stoke Field

St James's Palace
Whitehall Palace
Westminster Palace
Baynard's Castle
Chelsea Palace
Tower of London

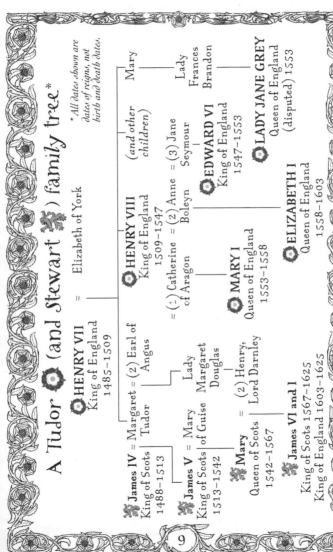

A Tudor 🌹 (and Stewart 🦁) family tree *

*All dates shown are dates of reigns, not birth and death dates.

HENRY VII = Elizabeth of York
King of England
1485–1509

James IV = Margaret = (2) Earl of
King of Scots Tudor   Angus
1488–1513

James V = Mary   Lady
King of Scots of Guise   Margaret Douglas
1513–1542

Mary = (2) Henry,
Queen of Scots Lord Darnley
1542–1567

James VI and I
King of Scots 1567–1625
King of England 1603–1625

Mary

HENRY VIII   (and other children)
King of England
1509–1547

= (1) Catherine = (2) Anne = (3) Jane
of Aragon   Boleyn   Seymour

Lady Frances Brandon

EDWARD VI
King of England
1547–1553

MARY I
Queen of England
1553–1558

ELIZABETH I
Queen of England
1558–1603

LADY JANE GREY
Queen of England
(disputed) 1553

9

Henry VII
Born 28 January 1457
Reigned 22 August 1485 – 21 April 1509

Henry VIII
Born 28 June 1491
Reigned 21 April 1509 – 28 January 1547

Edward VI
Born 12 October 1537
Reigned 28 January 1547 – 6 July 1553

Lady Jane Grey
Born 1536/7
Reigned 10–19 July 1553
Executed 12 February 1554

Mary I
Born 18 February 1516
Reigned 19 July 1553 – 17 November 1558

Elizabeth I
Born 7 September 1533
Reigned 17 November 1558 – 24 March 1603

INTRODUCTION

What *is* it about the Tudors?

hen it comes to drama, few royal families can match the Tudors. Want betrayals and back-stabbing, intrigues and scandals, bloody rebellions and gruesome executions? It's all here, against the glamorous backdrop of grand castles and lavish palaces, sumptuous feasts, gorgeous clothes and spectacular tournaments.

And what a cast of characters! Our tale begins with dark horse Henry VII, the rank outsider who battled against the odds to seize the crown and – even trickier – hold on to it. All that hard work paved the way for the legendary excesses of his son, Henry VIII, the larger-than-life monarch with a twinkle in his eye and a swagger in his step, who famously beheaded two wives and divorced two others. Henry's son and heir, Edward VI, may have been nicknamed the 'godly imp' for his saintly behaviour, but the fiendish antics of powerful nobles such as Edward Seymour and John Dudley ensured there was rarely a dull moment during the boy king's short reign – or after, when Lady Jane Grey ruled the country for a few brief days. The turmoil continued under 'Bloody' Mary, who undid everything her father had done and had hundreds burnt at the stake in the process. No less determined was her younger sister, Elizabeth I, 'Good Queen Bess', who defeated the mighty Armada and ruled over a colourful court of writers, poets and explorers.

In total, the five Tudors ruled for just 118 years. Yet some 500 years later, they remain among the best-known and most easily recognised of English monarchs – not least because Henry VIII and Elizabeth I left behind a string of splendid (and very flattering) portraits. The Tudors also did their best to spread the word that they were a bit special: poets such as Edmund Spenser linked them to legendary British kings such as Arthur, and Cadwaladr of Wales.[1]

Do the Tudors live up to their own hype? They were able, cunning, ambitious and ruthless. Henry VII greatly increased the power of the king and parliament by cracking down on lawless nobles, while Henry VIII's break with the Catholic Church was a turning point in English history. Elizabeth I's reign brought peace, stability, and a sense that England was a world power. England's merchants prospered under Tudor rule. The country grew into a great naval power while its sailors discovered many new lands. The court became a centre for the arts and sciences, and the works of William Shakespeare and others are still enjoyed today.

Enjoy the drama. But don't forget: for all their temper tantrums, excesses and cruelty, the Tudors knew how to get things done.

1. *Despite this, the Tudors generally played down their Welsh roots in order to emphasise their right to the English throne. Mary, for example, was known as 'the daughter of Henry VIII', rather than Mary Tudor.*

Bosworth Field, 1485: the last Plantagenet king bites the dust

CHAPTER ONE

The birth of a dynasty

or those who like their history bloody, the Tudor age began on 22 August 1485 when ambitious Welsh nobleman Henry Tudor, 2nd Earl of Richmond, thrashed King Richard III of England at the Battle of Bosworth Field in Leicestershire. As one dynasty kicked off, another ended – after Henry's victory, England waved goodbye to the Plantagenets who had ruled the country since the 12th century.

In Tudor times, the battle was portrayed as a clash of the titans: Saintly Henry versus

Wicked Richard. But in real life there were few saints in the dog-eat-dog world of medieval politics. The battle was won by a dirty trick played by knavish noble Lord William Stanley, who watched and waited from the wings with his 8,000 troops before deciding which side to join. When Henry rode towards Stanley asking for his support, Richard took a gamble. He charged down the hill at Henry's bodyguard, with 800 knights thundering along at his side.

Richard hoped to end the fight quickly by killing Henry. He hadn't bargained on the foul play of Lord Stanley, who suddenly attacked Richard from the flank. No wonder Richard was heard shouting, 'Treason, Treason!' Within a few minutes the battle was over. Though Richard almost cut his way through to Henry, he was now surrounded. Toppled from his horse, the last of the Plantagenets continued to fight on foot until he was cut down by Welsh spearmen.

The horrible hunchback?

King Richard III, Henry's opponent at Bosworth, is often depicted as a cruel, ugly villain, a ruthless tyrant. This all stems from the bad press he got in Tudor times from the likes of William Shakespeare and Sir Thomas More, when the royal court wanted to show how evil Richard was compared to Henry VII. But can we believe them?

- Richard was painted by Tudor artists as a hunchback with a withered arm and a limp. But these pictures were painted long after Richard's death – there's no sign of these deformities in earlier portraits or in records written at the time.

- Richard's famous line 'A horse, a horse, my kingdom for a horse!' was probably made up by Shakespeare, who wanted to show him as a coward. But brave Richard died fighting with a sword in his hand.

- OK, so Richard did grab the throne from his young nephew Edward V. But far from being a tyrant, Richard introduced many new laws that improved life for his subjects.

- In the traditional story of the murder of Edward V and his brother – the 'Little Princes in the Tower' – they're smothered to death by three of Richard's men, then buried in a shallow grave at the foot of a flight of stairs. The jury is still out on this one. Richard had already had the law changed so they couldn't come to the throne, so he had no need to kill them.

- Richard was also blamed for the death of his brother, George, duke of Clarence, who was allegedly drowned in a butt of Malmsey (a barrel of sweet wine) after a long drinking session at the Tower of London. Given that Clarence had just had a shouting match with King Edward IV (Richard's other brother), it's far more likely that Edward was behind his murder.

A night on the tiles was more than the duke of Clarence could handle.

No love lost

You may have heard a story about Henry's men finding Richard III's crown in a hawthorn bush.[1] True or not, Henry wasted no time in having himself crowned king on the battlefield. To make it clear who was boss, he had Richard's body stripped and lashed to a horse. In Leicester, the ex-king's naked corpse was displayed in a church for all to see, then buried in an unmarked grave two days later.

If that sounds a bit over the top, we should bear in mind that after years of bitter struggle Henry had a ruthless survival instinct that became a Tudor trademark. Now is probably a good time to wind back the clock and take a look at Henry's past. The squeamish among you can relax for a while, as even the Tudors had their romantic moments.

1. *A hawthorn bush became part of Henry's coat of arms, so there may be some truth in the tale.*

The long road to the top

Henry's granddad, Owen Tudor (in Welsh, Owain ap Maredudd ap Tewdwr),[2] had joined the household of English king Henry V as a pageboy. After winning his spurs at the Battle of Agincourt in 1415, he was promoted to the king's bodyguard. When Henry V died in 1422, Owen stayed on to guard the new king, 9-month-old Henry VI.

The dashing young squire soon caught the eye of the young king's mother, Catherine of Valois. According to a popular story of the time, she dressed up as one of her own ladies-in-waiting to play a trick on Owen when she heard he was chasing after one of her maids. She intended to scold him, but found herself falling head over heels in love. The couple may even have married in secret. The powerful duke of Gloucester, who ruled England on the baby king's behalf, did not approve. Owen was flung into Newgate prison in London and

2. In Welsh, ap means 'son of', so Henry was technically Henry ap Owain ap Maredudd ap Tewdwr. Henry was terribly proud of his ancestry, and claimed he was descended from the famous Welsh prince Cadwallader (Cadwaladr) the Great and even from Brutus, the mythical king of Britain and founder of London.

the queen was sent to a convent, where sadly she died the following year – by which time she had given Owen three sons. When Henry VI grew up he became good friends with his Tudor half-brothers. He made one of them, Edmund Tudor, earl of Richmond,[3] and in 1455 the king arranged Edmund's marriage to Lady Margaret Beaufort – a real catch, as she was a direct descendant of King Edward III.

Trouble was brewing, however. Henry VI's rule was being challenged by Richard, duke of York (later to become King Richard III). Civil war broke out between the Yorkists and Henry VI, leader of the house of Lancaster. Edmund Tudor, a supporter of Henry VI like his father, was taken prisoner less than a year later.[4] He died in Carmarthen Castle the following winter, leaving a 13-year-old widow who was by now seven months pregnant.

---

3. *Edmund's brother Jasper was created earl of Pembroke. We shall meet him again soon.*
4. *His father, Owen Tudor, had been released from prison by Henry VI and in 1461 led the Lancastrian forces at the Battle of Mortimer's Cross against Edward, earl of March. Defeated, Owen was captured and beheaded. Right to the end, his thoughts were of his beloved Catherine: 'The head which used to lie in the Queen's lap will now lie in the executioner's basket.'*

On 28 January 1457, Edmund's wife Margaret gave birth to her only child, Henry Tudor, in Pembroke Castle, Wales. For a while they stayed there under the protection of Henry's uncle Jasper Tudor, but soon after the Yorkist Edward IV seized the throne, his forces captured the castle. Some would have you believe that 4-year-old Henry Tudor was whisked away to live a secret life in the misty Welsh mountains – all very romantic, but in fact he probably grew up in the household of Yorkist Lord William Herbert, as the intended husband of Herbert's little daughter Maud.

Battle raged between the Houses of York and Lancaster. In 1470 the Earl of Warwick, known as the 'Kingmaker', restored Henry VI to the throne. Within a year, Edward IV recovered the crown after Warwick was slain at the Battle of Barnet. Henry VI was imprisoned in the Tower of London, where he died two months later, probably murdered on Edward's orders.

Confused? Well, imagine what it was like for little Henry, whose world was turned on its head after his protector William Herbert was executed for treachery.

As other royal heirs dropped like flies, Henry Tudor suddenly became a real contender for the throne, thanks to his mother's links to the royal family. He was no longer safe in Wales, so Uncle Jasper (only just back from exile himself) took Henry off to Brittany where they were taken in by Duke Francis. It would be 14 years before Henry returned to England. Hardened by the long years of exile and always fighting against the odds, young Henry grew up fast. A tall, athletic man with dark hair and fair skin, he was tough, determined, and ready for the challenges that lay ahead.

In the meantime, the Yorkists had started fighting each other. When Edward IV died in 1483, his unpopular brother made himself King Richard III and had several leading Yorkist barons beheaded. Around this time, Richard was suspected of having murdered his nephews in the Tower of London (see pages 17–18) – the final straw for many Yorkists who were already tired of Richard's rule. Soon they were plotting to bring young Henry Tudor to the throne, who had cleverly promised to patch things up with the Yorkists by marrying Elizabeth of York.

The secret Tudors

- **Roland de Velville.** Henry Tudor didn't spend all his time in Brittany thinking up fiendish schemes to win the throne. His French was a lot better than his English, and after Henry fell in love with a local girl, she bore him a son named Roland de Velville. After his father became Henry VII, Roland followed him to England and was made a knight after fighting at the Battle of Blackheath in 1497. Soon after, he became constable of Beaumaris Castle on the Isle of Anglesey in Wales, and married a Welsh woman. Very wisely, he kept his head down and never challenged the crown of his half-brother Henry VIII.

- **Henry Fitzroy.** King Henry VIII was apparently delighted when his affair with 'Bessie' Blount led to the birth of a son in 1519. He always looked after Bessie and granted her son his own household. At 16, handsome Henry Fitzroy married the duke of Norfolk's daughter, and for a short while he was even heir to the throne. He died in 1536, just before Edward VI was born.

- **Henry Carey.** In 1525, Henry VIII also had a brief affair with Mary Boleyn, the elder sister of Anne Boleyn. In 1526, Mary gave birth to a son, known as Henry Carey, who also died in 1536.

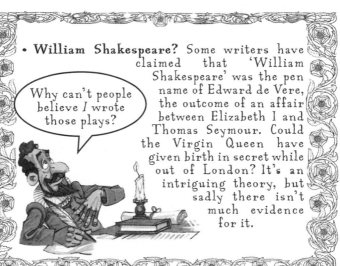

- **William Shakespeare?** Some writers have claimed that 'William Shakespeare' was the pen name of Edward de Vere, the outcome of an affair between Elizabeth I and Thomas Seymour. Could the Virgin Queen have given birth in secret while out of London? It's an intriguing theory, but sadly there isn't much evidence for it.

Why can't people believe I wrote those plays?

In September 1483, the exiled Henry was invited back to England by the Yorkist duke of Buckingham. When bad weather stalled the rebellion, Richard III bribed Duke Francis of Brittany to hand Henry over to him. In the nick of time, the Tudors caught wind of the plan and escaped to France (then a separate kingdom). They were soon joined by a gang of Yorkist rebels fleeing from England.

Henry Tudor charmed the French king Charles VIII into backing another invasion of England. By the summer of 1485, he had assembled an army of 2,000 men, mostly French and Scots mercenaries. Despite this foreign force, he had the backing of many powerful English nobles who were united in their hatred of Richard III.[5]

On 7 August 1485, Henry Tudor landed in his native Wales and marched east, joined by Lancastrian supporters. Surprisingly few Welshmen joined his army, but Henry did get the backing of the famous bard (traditional Welsh poet) Dafydd Llwyd ap Llywelyn, who had predicted that a Welsh king would one day appear to free his people from English rule. When Henry asked Dafydd to predict whether his expedition would end in defeat or triumph, Dafydd replied that he'd like to sleep on it before giving his answer. According to legend, the bard's wife advised him to predict success. If Henry became king, he would be rewarded;[6] if he was defeated, it wouldn't matter!

5. *Rumours were now circulating that Richard had cruelly poisoned his wife in order to marry his niece Elizabeth of York before Henry Tudor had the chance to do so.*
6. *Good call. When Henry became king, he made the bard a gentleman of his personal bodyguard.*

King at last

Henry's army marched 185 km (115 miles) in just eight days. Though Henry was heavily outnumbered when he faced Richard's forces at Bosworth, Lord Stanley's stab in the back swung the battle in his favour. Quick as he could, Henry had himself crowned (again) at Westminster Abbey, before Parliament had time to challenge his claim to the throne.[7] He then promptly married Elizabeth of York, combining the red rose emblem of York and the white rose of Lancaster into the Tudor rose.

The so-called Wars of the Roses had dragged on for 42 years. Though the actual fighting only amounted to about 18 months in all, a whole generation had been decimated. The English looked on in horror as the royal family chopped up their cousins and stuck their body parts on spikes all over the country. The Tudors used this to their advantage, threatening: 'If you don't obey us, it will only lead to another bloody civil war.'

7. As a distant relation of the royal family, Henry's main claim to the throne was the fact that God had given him victory on the field of battle!

Red dragon vs. white boar

The Wars of the Roses is a pretty name for a long, bloodthirsty struggle for the English crown. But the rose symbols that give the conflict its name (red for Lancaster, white for York) weren't worn much at the time. Most soldiers fought under their lord's banner, so Henry VII's forces at Bosworth fought under the Welsh red dragon, while the Yorkist army used Richard III's symbol of a white boar.

The red and white Tudor rose combines the colours of York and Lancaster.

Henry had finally made it to the top of the greasy pole. To stay there, he would have to work very hard as there were at least six Plantagenets with a better claim to the throne. Rarely calling Parliament, the new king relied on brute force to hang on to the crown. Though he retained several of Henry VI's advisors, he also brought in new faces such as Cardinal John Morton (his most trusted minister), Bishop Fox of Winchester, Richard Empson and Edmund Dudley.

At least there were now fewer barons around to kickstart a rebellion. Half the nobles in England had been wiped out during the Wars of the Roses – many were young men without an heir. Henry VII was in no rush to replace them. Knowing only too well how easily nobles swapped sides, he passed new laws banning the barons from building up large private armies. A court known as the Star Chamber had the power to arrest any nobles who broke the law. It also forced them to 'loan' large sums of money to the king. Anyone who had fought against Henry at Bosworth was declared a traitor, so the king could confiscate their lands and give them to his supporters.

The miracle king

Henry VII regarded himself as a lucky so-and-so – and he certainly survived against the odds to claim the throne. Once in power, he spun the line 'God is on my side', using prophecies, religious images and miracles to boost his image. Henry had to rely on such propaganda as he knew that others had a better claim to the throne. He also got Welsh bards to sing his praises: they cast him in the role of a returning avenger while slagging off Richard III as a murdering uncle.

Henry was right not to trust his nobles. In 1487 he crushed a revolt by the earl of Lincoln on behalf of Lambert Simnel, a young lad who claimed to be one of the missing princes from the Tower. Five years later, a Dutch boy named Perkin Warbeck made a similar claim, this time backed by Margaret of Burgundy, Edward IV's sister. Other plots simmered away, though none was a serious threat to Henry's rule.

The rivals

- The son of an Oxford baker, 10-year-old **Lambert Simnel** was proclaimed Edward VI in Dublin by Lord Kildare, the Lord Deputy of Ireland, in May 1487. Simnel was also backed by his alleged aunt Margaret of Anjou (widow of Henry IV), who sent 2,000 German mercenaries to help him. Did they believe his story? Probably not. They were just using him to get at Henry. The rebels were defeated at Stoke Field on 16 June 1487. Remarkably, Henry pardoned Simnel and gave him a job in the palace kitchens, where he lived for almost 40 years. Had Henry gone soft?

- **Perkin Warbeck**, the son of a Dutch tax collector, had some big hitters on his side, including the French king, the Holy Roman emperor, James IV of Scotland and Margaret of Burgundy. But after years of plotting, he was captured in 1497 when his invasion of England failed. After two years in the Tower of London, where he saw 'neither sun nor moon', Warbeck was executed for treason. That's more like a Tudor, Henry!

- **De la Pole brothers**. After John (named heir by Richard III) died fighting for Lambert Simnel, Edmund de la Pole became the leading Yorkist claimant to the throne until Henry VIII had him executed in 1513. The last remaining Pole, Richard, carried the flag until his death at the Battle of Pavia in 1525.

I'm a legend

Henry VII boasted that he was related to King Arthur, and named his first son after him. He first fell in love with the tales of the Knights of the Round Table while in Brittany. It's no coincidence that Sir Thomas Malory's version of the legend, *Le Morte d'Arthur*, was first printed by William Caxton in 1486, the year Prince Arthur was baptised. It was the first romance ever printed in English.

Henry was a smooth operator: while he walloped his nobles with taxes, he was more generous towards ordinary men and women. As a result, many of the rebels got a lot less support than they hoped for. Henry was also merciful and put to death only a handful of his enemies (unlike his son Henry VIII and granddaughter Elizabeth I). He solved many of England's problems overseas by diplomatic means. Lord Kildare, the former supporter of Lambert Simnel, ended up running Ireland for Henry, while a treaty with Scotland in 1502 ended a war that had rumbled on for 200 years.[8]

8. *The 'Treaty of Perpetual Peace' was backed up by the marriage of his daughter Margaret Tudor to James IV of Scotland. The treaty was broken in 1513 when James invaded England in support of the French.*

The year before, a treaty with Spain led to a wedding between Henry's 15-year-old son Arthur and Catherine of Aragon, the daughter of Ferdinand and Isabella of Spain. For years, the young couple exchanged love letters in Latin. Henry's plans were almost dashed by Arthur's death in 1502, just five months after the wedding.[9] Afraid he would have to pay back the large dowry, the king persuaded the Pope to allow Catherine to marry Arthur's younger brother, the future King Henry VIII.

Though Henry VII brought order and security to England after decades of chaos, he wasn't well-loved. His nobles grumbled at the hefty taxes. His minister Cardinal Morton is said to have come up with a sneaky scheme known as Morton's Fork. If a noble was a big spender, Morton argued, he could clearly afford to pay more taxes. If a lord lived simply and spent little, he must have money to spare for – you've guessed it – more taxes!

9. It had taken 13 years to arrange the marriage, partly due to haggling over money (worth 200,000 crowns to the royal coffers, or about £5 million today), but also due to worries over the stability of the Tudor dynasty. As the Spanish ambassador Dr Rodrigo de Puebla put it in 1488: 'Bearing in mind what happens to the kings of England every day, it is surprising that Ferdinand and Isabella dare think of giving their daughter at all.'

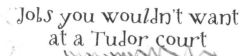

Jobs you wouldn't want at a Tudor court

- **Groom of the Stool.** Wiping the king's bottom was a plum job (should that be 'plumbing'?), as only the most trusted nobleman was allowed to get near the royal rump (most Tudor kings and queens were terrified of being bumped off). The main tool for the job was a diaper cloth woven in two different directions, which made it very absorbent. If your master got constipated, it was also your job to flush him out. Don't ask...

- **Gong farmer.** Another dirty job: there were no sewers in Tudor times, just large pits where human waste collected. As a gong farmer, you used a bucket and spade to clear up the mess and break up logjams. You were only allowed to work at night, by candlelight, and the filth you scraped up, known as 'night soil', had to be dumped outside the city walls. Mind you, the job was well paid and one of Elizabeth I's gong farmers, Samson, was paid partly in brandy.

> Since I took up this newfangled tobacco, I can hardly smell my work at all.

34

- **Headsman.** You needed a steady hand and a strong nerve to be an executioner, as the job was usually done in front of a large crowd. You were also public enemy no. 1, and though your face was covered by a mask everyone knew exactly who you were. At least the tips were good, as many nobles paid extra for a quick, neat job.

- **Spit-boy.** A Spanish visitor to the Tudor court in 1554 described the royal kitchens as a living hell. One of the worst jobs was turning huge chunks of meat as they slowly roasted on a spit over a fire. This was hot, dirty and mind-numbingly boring work. You had to dress properly too, as Henry VIII banned kitchen workers from going about naked or in ragged clothes. But if you were light-fingered, you never went hungry.

- **Dyers.** Though dyeing was a skilled job, Queen Elizabeth I wouldn't let you work within 8 km (5 miles) of her. Why? The woad used to dye clothes blue smelt like rotting cabbage. It stained your hands and even made your sweat blue!

- **Whipping boy.** The royal court kept a child who got whipped if the young prince did wrong. This doesn't sound like fun, but you got educated alongside the prince and shared his five-star lifestyle.

- **Weeder.** Women carried out the back-breaking work of making the royal gardens weed-free.

No expense spared

Henry VII was known for being a miser in his private life, but it didn't show in public. Throughout Europe, his court was known for its magnificence. Though Henry already lived in luxury in the palaces at Westminster, Greenwich and Eltham, he built a splendid new palace at Richmond, Surrey, with a round tower 124 steps high that offered a fabulous view of the surrounding countryside. Here the king held great banquets, where 700 guests or more were fed 60 dishes in a single meal. What better way to show off his new dynasty?

The Master of the Tents and Revels was responsible for staging eye-popping parties and entertainments at court. In November 1502, a dazzling display devised by composer William Cornish greeted the arrival of Catherine of Aragon in England. Knights paraded past the princess, some hidden inside a dragon escorted by a fancy-dress 'giant'. Others rode on a float decked out as a ship, with seamen firing cannon. That evening, a huge candlelit tower was hauled into the hall by men in seahorse costumes, escorted by ladies dressed as mermaids. It was some show. Such pageants left visiting princes in no doubt about Henry VII's great wealth.

The king didn't scrimp when it came to looking good, either. Compared with Louis XI, the 'Spider King' of France,[10] who wore rough, simple clothes, Henry looked absolutely fabulous in gold and silver cloth, luxurious furs and glittering jewellery. To complete the show, he kitted out his private bodyguard, the Yeomen of the Guard, in smart red and yellow uniforms. Henry also knew how to enjoy life. A keen huntsman, and with his own private zoo, Henry had a great love of music, which he passed on to his son Henry VIII. The first English king to build a library in his palace, he was an admirer of William Caxton, the first known printer in England, who had set up a press in Westminster in 1476.

With an eye for money-making ventures, Henry also funded Italian explorer John Cabot's voyage to North America in 1497.

10. *He earned this nickname by spinning a 'spider's web' of plots and intrigue.*

The royal bodyguard

The Yeomen of the Guard, formed by Henry VII, are still on duty on occasions such as the State Opening of Parliament, when they 'search' the cellars of the Palace of Westminster[11] – a tradition that dates back to the Gunpowder Plot of 1605, when Guy Fawkes and his associates tried to blow up Parliament. The oldest royal bodyguard in England, the Yeomen of the Guard are very proud of their heritage:

- Though they no longer carry the hagbuts (guns) or longbows of the original Yeomen Archers, they still wear Tudor-style uniforms that have changed little in over 520 years.

- If you want to annoy them, just confuse them with the Yeomen Warders who guard the Tower of London. Though their full-dress uniforms are similar, Yeomen of the Guard have cross belts, worn from the left shoulder.

- They also carry a sword and a pike known as a 'partisan', a reminder of the weapons used at the Battle of Bosworth Field.

- In the past, they carried a ceremonial axe when escorting prisoners from the Tower to trial at Westminster. If the prisoner was found guilty, the sharp edge of the axe was turned towards him or her on the return journey – a simple way of spreading the news.

11. *Nowadays the actual search is carried out by police officers.*

Henry's reputation for being mean probably stems from the gloomy mood at court following the sudden death of his son Arthur in 1502, closely followed by his wife Elizabeth less than two years later. Poor Henry was devastated, and though he thought about remarrying, his heart wasn't in it. Increasingly isolated, he was terrified of losing his eyesight as he liked to check the court papers himself and was afraid of being cheated.[12] Thanks to the insecurity of his early years, he never learned to trust even his closest friends.

Henry died on 21 April 1509 at Richmond Palace, a lonely and sad figure. His moment of glory had come at the very beginning of his reign. After that, it was all about peace and prosperity, and perhaps his biggest achievement was the fact that when Henry VIII came to the throne, there were no rivals lining up to snatch it from him.

I did it my way.

12. *Though he kept this a secret from everyone but his mother.*

Henry and the Pope didn't see eye to eye

CHAPTER TWO

Bluff King Hal

enry VIII, surely the most famous English monarch of all, was never meant to be king. Born in Greenwich Palace on 28 June 1491, Henry was the third child of Henry VII and Elizabeth of York, and grew up in the shadow of his elder brother, Arthur, Prince of Wales. Henry was all set for a life in the Church: no playboy antics, no parties, no six wives and no lopping people's heads off.

As a result, young Henry was expected to study hard. He was taught by a priest called John Skelton, a famous poet and musician who encouraged the prince's love of music. Henry also had a good ear for language and became fluent in Latin, French and Spanish. Later on in life, he spent many evenings discussing astronomy, science and religion with his minister Thomas More. But Henry, just like his father, also loved stories about knights in armour battling fierce giants.

Even as a child, Henry had a team of servants scampering around him, including minstrels and a fool called John Goose. All in all, he was spoilt rotten and, as you can imagine, at times he was a little monster.

In 1502, Arthur died from a mysterious illness at the age of 15. Suddenly, 10-year-old Henry was thrust into the limelight as the new heir to the throne.

Arthur   Henry

Yes, Majesty!

Some boys like to collect stamps or fossils. Henry VIII collected titles:

- Aged 2: Constable of Dover Castle and Lord Warden of the Cinque Ports.

- Aged 3: Knight of the Bath and Duke of York.

- Aged 4: Knight of the Garter.

- Aged 13: Prince of Wales, following the death of his elder brother Arthur.

- Henry was later made Lord Lieutenant of Ireland, and in 1542, King of Ireland. (The Irish were not consulted about this.)

- Ironically, the title of Defender of the Faith was given to Henry as a young man after he defended Pope Leo X against the Protestant Martin Luther. He called Luther 'a great limb of the Devil'. Luther responded by calling Henry 'a mad fool with a frothy mouth' and the 'king of lies'. Even after the split with Rome, Henry hung on to the title, which to this day is used by English kings and queens and can be seen on banknotes and coins.

- With all those titles, what would you call him? Around 1519, Henry decided he should be called 'Majesty' as well as 'Highness' and 'Grace', even in official documents.

Arthur had been married to Princess Catherine of Aragon,[1] and to ensure the alliance with Spain, young Henry took his place and was engaged to the princess just 14 months after Arthur's death.[2] Given that she had no choice in the matter, Catherine could have done a lot worse: as a teenager, her new hubby was handsome, charming and sporty.

At 6 ft 2 in (1.88 m) tall, Henry towered over most of his subjects,[3] and his broad shoulders must have made him seem all the more regal. He had blue eyes, very fair skin, and red hair which he wore in a bob. One court visitor said, 'Nature could not have done more for him.' Another described him as 'the most handsomest potentate [ruler] I ever set eyes on'. Henry's calves were considered very sexy and his dancing was much admired: 'He leaps like a stag,' remarked one onlooker.

1. The youngest child of King Ferdinand II of Aragon and Queen Isabella I of Castile, who had funded Columbus' voyage to the New World in 1492.
2. In order for Henry to marry his brother's wife, he had to get permission from the Pope. Under pressure from Henry and Queen Isabella, the Pope finally agreed after Catherine swore she had been wedded but not bedded by Arthur. The actual marriage didn't take place until just before Henry's coronation, by which time he was 17.
3. In those days, the average Londoner was 5 ft 5 in (1.65 m).

A man of many talents

- **Musician.** At the age of 10, Henry could already play the fife, harp, viol and drums. Later he owned a vast collection of instruments including 26 lutes, 10 trombones, 14 trumpets, 5 bagpipes, 76 recorders and 78 flutes. Songs which may have been composed by Henry include 'Hélas, madame', 'Pastime with good company' (see page 7) and, allegedly, 'Greensleeves' (pages 178–179). The king also liked to sing. Two of his favourite songs were 'By the banks as I lay' and 'As I walked the wood so wild'.

- **Archer.** Henry showed off his skill at the Field of the Cloth of Gold (see page 56) by hitting a bullseye from 240 yards (220 m) – though in later life he needed glasses to read.

- **Knight.** One of the best jousters in the country, Henry took on all comers along with his brother-in-law, Charles Brandon, duke of Suffolk, who like the king was a giant bear of a man.

- **Wrestler.** Henry was a skilled wrestler, though he never quite got over his defeat by King Francis I of France, who threw him with a move known as a 'flying mare'.

- **Gambler.** Henry was mad keen on cock-fighting and had his own pit built at Whitehall Palace.

- **Tennis player.** By 1530 Henry had built indoor tennis courts at four of his favourite palaces: Greenwich, St James's, Hampton Court and Whitehall. Supposedly the king was in the middle of a game when the bloody head of Anne Boleyn was brought to him.

- **Skittle player.** Henry enjoyed skittles so much that he took a portable bowling alley with him to France. He also loved bowls, though he banned poor people from playing the game as he believed they should practise fighting skills such as archery instead.

Good shot, Your Grace!

The real thing
The version of tennis that Henry played is now called 'real tennis', from the Old French word for 'royal'.

The playboy king

'Bluff King Hal' was already a big hit with the people of England when he came to the throne in 1509. Cheering crowds lined the streets during his coronation on 24 June, 13 days after his marriage to Catherine.

Henry soon made his mark, employing a tactic he was to use again and again: when anyone stood in his way, he simply had them charged with treason and executed. First on the chopping block were two nobles who had been loyal servants to his father: Sir Edmund Dudley and Sir Richard Empson were arrested just two days after his coronation and executed shortly after.

But Henry didn't knuckle down to the serious business of running the country. He was too busy having fun. The king had an enormous appetite for life. He wanted his court to be the envy of Europe, a magnet for scholars and artists. A talented musician, author and poet, Henry loved being surrounded by the brightest and best minds. His glittering court became an endless round of hunting, feasting, dancing and gambling.[4] In 1519 he got a slap on the wrist from the Privy Council after hanging out with the young bloods at court. Apparently, they had encouraged him to slip into London in disguise and behave 'in a foolish manner'!

The king spent only a couple of hours a day on matters of state; he found writing 'somewhat tedious and painful'.[5] That said, he was still very much the boss. He kept his ministers on their toes, thanks to his often cruel and ruthless personality and his tendency to change policy in the blink of an eye.

Yet the king could turn on the charm when he needed to, whether talking to court ladies,[6] common people or foreign ambassadors. He could remember the name of every servant employed in all the royal households. Fit and trim, he had great energy, sometimes chasing stags for 28 miles (45 km) without stopping.[7]

4. Henry lost hundreds of pounds to his courtiers, some of whom brought in professional gamblers from France and Italy to help them fleece the king.
5. Though you wouldn't believe it if you saw his long love letters to Anne Boleyn, now in the Vatican Museum.
6. Apparently he never failed to take his hat off to a lady.
7. In a single day in 1541, Henry and his courtiers shot 200 deer.

Henry's arty friends

- **Sir Thomas Wyatt the Elder** (1503-1542). A celebrated poet and courtier, Wyatt had a flair for writing love poetry. In 1536 he was one of several men accused of having an affair with Anne Boleyn; he was sent to the Tower of London, but was lucky enough to be pardoned.

- **Desiderius Erasmus** (1466-1536). The renowned Dutch thinker spent five years at Henry's court. He claimed that Henry was the model Christian king.

- **John Heywood** (c.1497-c.1580) was one of the first English playwrights to write comedies, or 'interludes'. He also worked as a minstrel and a jester at Henry's court.

- **Hans Holbein the Younger** (c.1498-1543). The great German painter is best known for his portraits of the rich and famous at Henry's court. After Jane Seymour died, Henry sent Holbein around Europe to paint pictures of potential brides. Holbein's picture of Anne of Cleves was said to be rather flattering, and Henry regretted his choice.

- **Will Somers** (d.1560). The best-known of Henry's court jesters, Somers eventually retired in the reign of Elizabeth I. It was said that in the king's later years, when he was in constant pain from leg ulcers, only Somers could lift the king's spirits.

Off to war

All of Henry's athletic hobbies were practice for the real thing – war. Henry had his sights set on both Scotland and France (no doubt egged on by his Spanish wife). In 1513, he invaded France and defeated a French army at the Battle of the Spurs. In the same year, the Earl of Surrey led the force that defeated and killed James IV of Scotland, an old ally of France, at the Battle of Flodden Field.

England was a small nation compared to France or Spain, the two major powers in Europe, though it was relatively wealthy thanks to the wool trade.[8] But Henry VIII was a born wheeler-dealer and made the most of shifting alliances – helped by Cardinal Wolsey, who played France and the Holy Roman Empire against each other. By the end of Henry's reign, England was a power to be reckoned with. Nevertheless, most Europeans looked down on the English. One Spanish visitor described them as 'pink, pasty and quarrelsome'.

8. *Wool profits built the magnificent Tudor churches of East Anglia and the West Country.*

Hungry for a fight

Napoleon once said that 'An army marches on its stomach,' and Henry VIII would have heartily agreed. The king took 200 kitchen staff with him to feed him while on campaign, and the royal kitchens were kept well stocked by a train of wagons which included:

- poultry wagon
- mobile bakery
- wine wagon
- sweet/confectionery wagon
- fresh-food larder.

In contrast, the rest of the English army lived on a simple diet of beef, biscuits and beer. Of these, beer was by far the most important – even at court, more beer was drunk than wine. During a campaign in Spain in 1512, Henry's thirsty army refused to fight when they were offered wine or cider instead of beer, and their commander was forced to bring them home!

England at this time was a dangerous, violent place, full of plots and intrigue. Punch-ups were common at meetings of the Privy Council, and Henry VIII sometimes thumped ministers who disagreed with him. Even church leader Cardinal Wolsey was known for his foul language, and he once came to blows with a mission sent by the Pope himself. The common people were regarded as drunken and loud-mouthed, and were famous for hating foreigners.

Though Henry won several battles, he never achieved a decisive victory against his rivals Francis I of France or Charles V of the Holy Roman Empire.[9] Hot-blooded Henry was no coward and liked to lead from the front, unlike many other kings of the time. During one siege he deliberately taunted the defending French cannons by riding up and down in front of them in his finest gold tunic and red feathered cap.

9. The grandly named Holy Roman Empire was a collection of states in Central Europe covering what is now Germany, Austria, the Czech Republic, Switzerland, the Netherlands, Belgium, Luxembourg and Slovenia, as well as parts of France, Italy and Poland – in short, a force to be reckoned with.

Gun nut

Cannons and gunpowder revolutionised warfare during the 16th century. By the time of Henry's last war in 1544, small firearms known as 'hagbuts' were being used by English soldiers. Henry was obsessed with the latest hi-tech gadgets and loved to show off his collection of weapons and armour, which included exotic archery equipment, 2,250 pieces of artillery and 6,500 handguns. Within a few years of Henry's reign the Tower of London held so many guns that a visitor noted: 'Hell itself could not resist so powerful a force.'

The collection, now split between the Tower and the Royal Armouries Museum in Leeds, is still one of Britain's major tourist attractions.

Henry's impressive collection included this bizarre horned helmet, part of a suit of armour given to him early in his reign.

Going to war was never straightforward, however. First, Henry had to drum up enough money to pay for an army, especially as he often relied on mercenaries (hired professional soldiers) to make up the numbers. Even when a campaign was going well, bad weather could halt an army in its tracks. In 1523 the English army was just 44 miles (70 km) from Paris when temperatures plummeted. Over 100 of Henry's men froze to death while others watched their nails drop off from frostbite.

Henry VIII particularly wanted to follow in the footsteps of his hero Henry V, who had crushed the French at Agincourt a hundred years earlier in 1415. Francis I was equally ambitious, and neither trusted the other. Henry had good reason, as one of his spies found out that Francis was in cahoots with the traitor Richard de la Pole.[10] De la Pole was in Brittany with 12,000 mercenaries all set to invade England. Henry decided to nip the problem in the bud by making peace with the French king.

10. See page 31. Richard de la Pole was nicknamed The White Rose as he was a Yorkist.

Henry takes it on the chin

- Most men in Tudor times were clean-shaven before King Henry VIII set the style for beards and moustaches.

- Before going to France, Henry told the French ambassador he would stop shaving so he and Francis I could compare beards. In the end, Catherine of Aragon persuaded him to shave it off.

- In 1535, having divorced Catherine, Henry finally began to wear a beard permanently and cut his hair short, ordering his courtiers to follow suit.

- Henry washed his hair just three or four times a year with water and wood ash.

> I'm such a handsome devil.

- His favourite perfume was a mix of musk, ambergris and civet.[11]

11. *Ambergris is a grey marine substance sometimes found in the stomachs of whales, musk is made from the scent glands of wild deer, while civet is taken from a pouch under the tails of male and female civet cats.*

Henry and Francis planned a great tournament known as the Field of the Cloth of Gold[12] to show off their wealth and majesty. The event, held in June 1520, became the talk of Europe. Henry paid 6,000 workers to build a mock palace, while Francis erected a beautiful pavilion.[13] The tournament lasted three weeks and there were great feasts and jousting every day. Though Henry had his nose put out of joint when he lost a wrestling match with the small but slippery Francis, both went away feeling they were top dog. Henry then headed straight for the court of Charles V to plot an alliance against Francis, and two years later his soldiers were ravaging northern France. So much for all the hugs and kisses between the two monarchs.

Henry was also set on building a formidable English navy, following on from his father Henry VII who had built two of the largest warships in the world, the *Regent* and the *Sovereign*. By the end of his reign, Henry VIII had a fleet of 80 ships. His pride and joy, the *Great Harry* or *Henry Grâce à Dieu*, weighed

12. *Named after the gold cloth used to decorate many of the luxurious tents that were created specially for the occasion.*
13. *Henry was delighted when this blew away mid-tournament.*

1,000 tonnes and carried 400 soldiers along with a crew of 300. It wasn't all plain sailing, though – on 19 July 1545 the great warship *Mary Rose* sank before Henry's eyes when a gust of wind caught the ship sideways while the gun ports were open. The water poured in and the *Mary Rose* sank like a stone. Most of the 500 crew drowned.

The loss of the *Mary Rose*

Today, the remains of the ship are preserved in Portsmouth as a Tudor time capsule.

The King's Great Matter

As a young man, Henry had married
Catherine of Aragon to honour his father's
dying wish to form an alliance between
England and Spain. Though Catherine had
given birth to a daughter, Mary (later Queen
Mary I), in 1516, she was now getting a bit
long in the tooth to give Henry the son and
heir he wanted so desperately.[14] Henry feared
there would be a civil war if a queen rather
than a king succeeded him. The whole topic
wound up Henry so much that it became
known as the king's 'Great Matter'.

Henry gave the job of getting an annulment
(a declaration that the marriage was not valid)
to Cardinal Thomas Wolsey (1473–1530),
leader of the Catholic Church in England.
From 1514 to 1529, Wolsey was Lord
Chancellor, and virtually ran the kingdom
while his master hunted, partied until dawn
and wrote love songs. Henry also used Wolsey
to keep an eye on possible rivals for the crown,
including Henry's own friend Edward

14. A son, Henry, duke of Cornwall, had been born in 1511 but lived
only a few weeks.

Stafford, duke of Buckingham, who was one of the richest and most powerful nobles in England (and a descendant of Edward III). In 1521, when Wolsey accused Stafford of planning to murder the king with a knife hidden in a cloak, there could only be one outcome. Stafford was beheaded at Tower Hill, while all his lands and property went to the crown.

Wolsey lived like a king in his magnificent palace at Hampton Court, dressing in a velvet cloak with a heavy gold chain hanging around his neck.[15] Many people, including Henry's old teacher John Skelton, thought that Wolsey was getting far too big for his boots (he came from a humble background). As well as being jealous of Wolsey's new-found wealth, many older nobles were annoyed that he had reduced their power while increasing the authority of courts such as the Star Chamber. They were also furious that he forced them to provide loans to pay for the king's foreign wars.

15. When the French ambassador came to visit in 1527, Hampton Court had 280 rooms and silver and gold plate worth some £75,000,000 in today's money. However, most of Wolsey's palace was rebuilt once Henry got his hands on it.

Top ten palaces

Henry began with a dozen palaces and died with almost 60. Here are some of his favourites:

- **Greenwich.** Henry's birthplace and probably his favourite palace. Like a Tudor amusement park, it offered tennis, archery, bear baiting, cock fighting, hunting and hawking.

- **Whitehall.** Like Hampton Court (below), this was grabbed from Cardinal Wolsey after his downfall. The palace was once the largest building in the world, with some 1,500 rooms. Today just a tiny part of the Tudor palace survives, next to No. 10 Downing St, official home of the British Prime Minister.

- **Eltham.** The king spent a happy childhood here. Though most of the original palace is gone, the Great Hall survives.

- **Tower of London.** Henry lived here during the first days of his reign in April 1509. It also stored his huge collection of arms.

- **Hampton Court.** A 'gift' from Cardinal Wolsey, this was massively rebuilt by the king, who wanted at least one palace big enough to hold his entire court. The astronomical clock added in 1540 still works!

- **Leeds Castle, Kent.** Though he only spent a few days there, Henry spent a fortune turning this fairytale castle into a luxurious home for his first wife, Catherine of Aragon. He also strengthened its defences, fearing an invasion by Spain or France.

- **St James.** This red-brick palace was built by Henry VIII on the site of a former leper hospital. Its gatehouse still survives. Mary I died here and her heart and bowels were buried in the palace's Chapel Royal.

- **Nonsuch Palace, Surrey.** Built from scratch, this spectacular palace cost a whopping £24,000 to build (equivalent to £104 million today), though it wasn't finished when the king died. It was pulled down in the 1680s to pay off the gambling debts of one of King Charles II's mistresses.

- **Baynard's Castle.** Henry VII changed the castle from a fortress to a palace, and Catherine of Aragon, Anne Boleyn and Anne of Cleves all lived here at different times.

- **Hatfield House.** Used by Henry as a home for his children, Edward, Elizabeth and Mary. Elizabeth was staying here in 1558 when she heard that she had become Queen.

Henry's other homes included: Windsor Castle, Dover Castle, Westminster Palace, Beaulieu Palace (Essex), Knole, Woodstock, Richmond (Surrey), and the castles of Raglan, Hever, Farnham, Chester, Ludlow, Pontefract and Pembroke.

The break with Rome

Pope Clement VII refused to grant Henry an annulment. After six years Henry could wait no longer, and secretly married a young lady-in-waiting, Anne Boleyn. This was a very big deal. Despite his playboy image, Henry was a good Catholic who prayed every day.[16] When the Pope excommunicated him, it meant that Henry's soul could never go to heaven. For a believer, this is just about the scariest thing that can happen to you.

In 1533, Henry solved the problem by creating the Protestant Church of England, joining other churches in Europe that had broken away from the Pope. As head of his very own church, he could make his divorce legal.[17] The split from Rome wasn't just about a new wife and improving his chances of having a son and heir. Henry didn't like having to obey a Pope (effectively an Italian baron), and the split also gave him the perfect excuse to plunder rich Catholic monasteries and seize their land.

16. Despite the break with the Pope, Henry hated Protestant radicals who wanted to do away with Catholic beliefs, and he had many of them burnt as heretics from 1539 until the end of his reign.
17. To this day, the head of the Church of England is the king or queen.

Snakes and ladders at court

• **Thomas Wolsey** (c.1472–1530)

Up: The son of a poor Ipswich butcher, by 1515 Wolsey was both a cardinal and Lord Chancellor. Almost as rich as the king, he employed almost 1,000 people and lived in great luxury at Hampton Court (pictured).

Down: Wolsey's failure to get the king a divorce led to his sacking in October 1529. He would probably have been executed if he hadn't died en route from York to London on 24 November 1530.

• **Thomas More** (1478–1535)

Up: Trained as a lawyer, More was also a wily statesman and a celebrated scholar. His book on politics, *Utopia*, was a best-seller. More was knighted in 1521, and followed Wolsey as Lord Chancellor in 1529.

Down: More, a man of firm principles, was against the break with Rome (he also stayed away from Anne Boleyn's coronation). He finally fell out of favour with the king after he refused to acknowledge Henry as supreme head of the Church of England. He was executed on 6 July 1535.

• Thomas Cromwell (1485–1540)

Up: The son of a Putney blacksmith, clever Cromwell rose through the ranks to become Henry's chief minister in 1534. A ruthless politician who made many enemies, Cromwell was behind the king's decision to make himself head of the English Church.

Down: In 1540, Cromwell pushed Henry VIII into marrying Anne of Cleves. When the marriage ended in disaster, his political opponents encouraged the king to have him arrested. Cromwell was beheaded on 28 July 1540, though in later life the king bitterly regretted ordering his death.

• Thomas Cranmer (1489–1556)

Up: Cranmer caught the king's attention in 1529 when he supported the break with Rome. In 1533 he became archbishop of Canterbury and granted the king a divorce from Catherine of Aragon. He later wrote the *Book of Common Prayer*, the basis of all services in the Church of England.

Down: Cranmer survived Henry's reign, despite several plots against him in the 1540s. However, he was burned as a heretic by Mary I on 21 March 1556.

• Richard Rich (1496–1567)

Up: A thoroughly nasty piece of work, Rich became Henry's top legal advisor and carried out his dirty work, such as extracting confessions from the king's political enemies. He played an important part in the downfall of both More and Cromwell.

Down: A man of few principles, Rich skilfully moved with the times. He became a baron under Edward VI and later helped Mary round up heretics.

• Stephen Gardiner (1495–1555)

Up: Gardiner became Henry's chief secretary and helped in his divorce from Catherine of Aragon, after which the king made him bishop of Winchester. After the fall of Cromwell he played an important role in foreign affairs.

Down: Gardiner was against the break from Rome, and he spent five years in the Tower during Edward VI's reign. His career was revived under Mary, however, and he negotiated her marriage to Philip II of Spain.

When Henry had first fallen for Anne Boleyn, she pushed the king away,[18] but this only made him more obsessed with her. She demanded to be queen, which gave Henry further reason to leave Catherine of Aragon. Anne knew timing was everything, and she encouraged Henry to dismiss Cardinal Wolsey after he failed to get a speedy divorce.

Henry had often forced nobles to hand over prime properties, and Wolsey hoped to win back the king's favour by giving him Hampton Court Palace. He failed. In 1530, when Wolsey was found plotting against Anne with Queen Catherine and the Pope, he was arrested and died in custody. It was a warning to anyone else who didn't give the king exactly what he wanted.

With Wolsey gone, Anne made the most of her position. She even had her family chaplain, Thomas Cranmer, appointed archbishop of Canterbury. Meanwhile Henry made Thomas More his new Lord Chancellor. More was clever and honest – but he didn't support Henry's split with the Pope. When another

18. *'I beseech Your Highness most earnestly to desist… I would rather lose my life than my honesty.'*

friend of Anne's, the lawyer Thomas Cromwell, tried to introduce new laws which recognised Henry's power over the Church, More resigned. Like so many before him, More was soon for the chop. His last words to the executioner were: 'Pluck up thy spirits, man, and be not afraid, my neck is very short.'[19] And, not surprisingly, Anne's man Cromwell now became Henry's chief minister.

The break with the Pope led to the biggest land grab in English history. Smaller monasteries, friaries and convents went first, in 1536. The bigger fish were scooped up four years later. Henry used the land and wealth grabbed from the monasteries to reward his barons and keep them loyal. To strengthen his grip on the new church, he stamped out traditional practices such as pilgrimage and belief in miracles, and ordered the destruction of images, relics and shrines. He encouraged the idea that his power was linked to the Ten Commandments. In effect, anything he said was the word of God, which made it almost impossible for anyone to disagree with him.

19. Thomas More was joined on Tower Hill by the bishop of Rochester, who had also defied Henry. Any monks who refused to join the new church were tortured and executed.

The six wives at a glance

1. Catherine of Aragon DIVORCED
  (1485–1536)
Motto: Humble & Loyal.
Nickname: The Queen of
  Earthly Queens.
How it happened: Henry VII's choice, part of a
  political alliance with Spain.
Looks: Good-looking, with fair skin, blue eyes
  and strawberry-blond hair, though under 5 ft
  (1.52 m) tall.
Plus points: Charming and gracious. Got on
  well with Henry as they both loved books and
  hunting.
Minus points: Stubborn and proud. When the
  marriage ended, she refused to go quietly.
How long did it last?: Married 1509–1533.
Why did it end?: Henry had the marriage
  annulled because she couldn't give him a son.
Curiosity: While her body was being embalmed,
  a black growth was found on her heart –
  probably a sign of cancer rather than poison.

2. Anne Boleyn BEHEADED
  (mid-1500s–1536)
Motto: The Most Happy.
Nickname: Goggle Eyes.
How it happened: Lady-in-waiting
  to Catherine of Aragon, first spotted by
  Henry in 1526, after he had already had an
  affair with her sister Mary.
Looks: Very glamorous, with olive skin, dark
  eyes, dark hair and a long, elegant neck.

Plus points: Clever, strong-willed, independent and a lover of music. Playing hard to get for six years made Henry mad with desire. She was a fabulous dresser.

Minus points: All those clothes cost a fortune. She was possibly too clever and often argued with the king.

How long did it last?: Married 1533–1536.

Why did it end?: Henry had her beheaded. Anne was accused of having lovers, but the real reason was the lack of a son.

Curiosity: According to one later writer, she had a sixth finger on one hand; her enemies claimed that this proved she was a witch!

3. Jane Seymour
(1508/9–1537)

DIED

Motto: Bound to Obey & Serve.

Nickname: Tudor Rose.

How it happened: Lady-in-waiting to Catherine of Aragon and Anne Boleyn, first spied by Henry in 1536.

Looks: Not her strong point. Pale and blonde.

Plus points: She gave the king a son (Edward VI), and instantly became Henry's favourite queen. Good at needlework and running the household – just what Henry wanted.

Minus points: Has been described as a doormat. Not as educated as Catherine or Anne (though this suited Henry).

How long did it last?: Married 1536–1537.

Why did it end?: Jane died from an infection after Edward's birth. Henry was gutted.

Curiosity: She was King Henry's fifth cousin three times removed.

4. Anne of Cleves

DIVORCED

(1515–1557)

Motto: God Send Me Well to Keep.

Nicknames: Flanders Mare; later, The King's Beloved Sister.

How it happened: Selected for the king by Thomas Cromwell, though the king got to see her portrait.

Looks: Tall, slim, with dark hair. No great beauty, but not as ugly as Henry made out.

Plus points: Gentle, sweet-natured and liked playing cards – actually a good match for Henry. Once they were divorced, she became good friends with the king.

Minus points: Shy and awkward, not helped by the fact that she only spoke German. Henry complained of her 'evil smells'. She found the king equally unattractive.

How long did it last?: Married January–July 1540.

Why did it end?: Henry divorced her because he couldn't bear to sleep with her.

Curiosities: According to one story, at their first meeting Henry kissed her while in disguise and she rejected his kiss.

5. Catherine Howard

BEHEADED

(c.1521–1542)

Motto: No Other Wish Than His.

Nicknames: Kitty, Rose Without a Thorn.

How it happened: Maid of honour for Anne of Cleves, spotted in 1539.

Looks: Hard to say, as Henry had most of her portraits burnt – not amazingly beautiful.

Plus points: Flirtatious, sweet and incredibly charming. Young, too – which was ideal as Henry hoped to father several more sons.

Minus points: Immature and foolish. Several previous affairs. Repulsed by Henry's obesity.

How long did it last?: Married 1540–1542.

Why did it end?: Beheaded, after Henry found out about her affair with Thomas Culpeper (at first the king wanted to kill her himself).

Curiosity: Her ghost is said to haunt Hampton Court Palace, banging on doors and screaming Henry's name.

6. Catherine Parr
(1512–1548)

SURVIVED

Motto: To Be Useful in All that I Do.

Nickname: Kind Mother Kate.

How it happened: She worked for Henry's daughter Mary. They met in 1542.

Looks: Petite and pretty, with red hair and grey eyes.

Plus points: Kind, intelligent, caring companion for an ageing king. Loving stepmother to his children. First English queen to write a book (*Prayers or Meditations*, 1545).

Minus points: Already courting Sir Thomas Seymour and probably in love with him. She married Seymour soon after Henry's death.

How long did it last?: Married 1543–1547

Why did it end?: Henry died, making Catherine the only wife to survive him.

Curiosities: She carried licorice and cinnamon lozenges to keep her breath sweet. When her coffin was opened in the 18th century, some of her flesh was still white and moist.

A son and heir

Meanwhile, things started to turn sour for Anne Boleyn. Few cheered at her coronation, and some onlookers apparently looked so glum they could have been at a funeral. It was certainly no fun for Anne, who was already heavily pregnant. She kept having to go to the toilet, and two ladies hid under the table with a pot for any emergencies. To many people, Anne was still the king's mistress and not fit to be queen. They called her nasty nicknames such as 'Goggle Eyes'. Henry himself found that bright, capable Anne was far too independent for his liking, and her furious temper matched his own.

Henry was also impatient for a son and heir. When Anne gave birth to Elizabeth in 1533, he was bitterly disappointed. In 1536 she lost another baby,[20] predicted to be a boy by the court astrologers. Henry accused her of having other lovers – including her brother! Five men were arrested. One of them, Mark

20. *A very common occurrence in Tudor times when so little was known about medicine or even basic hygiene. Between them, Catherine of Aragon and Anne Boleyn had ten pregnancies. From these, only two children, Mary and Elizabeth, survived.*

Smeaton, confessed on the rack (who wouldn't?), and Anne's fate was sealed. Unlike Catherine of Aragon, she had no royal supporters to protect her. On 2 May 1536 Anne was arrested and taken to the Tower of London. She was accused of adultery and high treason. Inevitably, she was found guilty and executed 17 days later.[21]

Never one for hanging about, Henry secretly became engaged the day after Anne Boleyn's execution, to Jane Seymour, one of Anne's ladies-in-waiting. The couple tied the knot ten days later. Henry got on much better with Jane than with Anne, perhaps because she never made the mistake of disagreeing with him. In 1537 Jane gave birth to a son, Prince Edward. Henry was over the moon. Bonfires were lit around the country, church bells rang and 2,000 cannon shots were fired from the Tower of London. But the celebrations didn't last long: when Jane died 12 days later from an infection, Henry was grief-stricken.

21. *The execution took place inside the Tower, perhaps because the king dreaded what she might say in public before she died. He needn't have worried: her final words described him as a 'godly, noble and gentle prince'.*

Troubled times

When it came to money, Henry and his father were like chalk and cheese. Financially, the reign of Henry VIII was a near-disaster. Even though he had inherited a thriving economy from his father and then topped up the royal coffers with loot stolen from the monasteries, Henry gambled away a fortune and spent huge sums on foreign wars. To cut his losses, he began to mint poor-quality silver coins. The thin layer of silver on the surface soon wore away, often on the nose of the king's image, revealing the cheap copper below. As a result, Henry was given the nickname 'Coppernose'.

Coins of Henry VIII
from the wreck of the *Mary Rose*

Hey, big spender

Grand palaces, lavish parties and spectacular tournaments all cost a fortune. But the spending didn't stop there...

- Henry spent huge sums of money on clothing each year. He ordered 79 gowns during his reign, along with a wardrobe full of bonnets, which he adored. Like any self-respecting fashion victim, Henry also owned lots of shoes, including football and hunting boots.

- In three years, he splashed out the equivalent of £165,000 on gifts for Anne Boleyn.

- Henry's food bill must have made the court treasurer weep. In one year the king and his guests ate 8,200 sheep, 2,330 deer, 2,870 pigs, 1,240 oxen, 24,000 larks and 33,000 chickens. Gulp!

- Henry owned over 2,000 tapestries (though 400 of these were inherited from his father). Twenty-eight of them are still hanging at Hampton Court.

- Henry's palaces were stuffed with fine furniture. His giant bed, made from walnut wood, took six men 10 months to carve before it was covered in gold leaf. The royal toilet or 'stool' was covered in the softest sheep and calf skins, decorated in black velvet and silk ribbons, and had its own leather carrying case.

The year 1536 was a crunch time for Henry. His popularity had already taken a dive as rich and poor alike got fed up with paying heavy taxes.[22] The practice of enclosure (grabbing public land by fencing it in) made many others hopping mad. Meanwhile Henry's new church was hated by many believers, especially in the north. A small-scale revolt in Lincolnshire developed into a widespread rising against the new religious ideas, known as the Pilgrimage of Grace. Some 40,000 rebels, a curious mix of nobles and peasants, marched on Lincoln and later York, demanding the freedom to worship as Catholics.

For the first time in Henry's reign, there was a serious threat to the throne. The king dealt with it in his usual no-nonsense way. He promised to pardon the rebels and invited their leader, Robert Aske, a one-eyed Lincolnshire laywer, to a royal banquet. Never having met Henry, Aske assumed the king would keep his word, naïvely blaming Henry's 'evil counsellors' for the reforms. We can only imagine Aske's surprise and horror when

22. They weren't fooled by cheery names such as the Amicable Grant and the Friendly Tax.

the treacherous Henry had him flung into the Tower. He was charged with treason and executed, along with over 200 rebels.[23] Many others who kept to the old faith wisely decided to keep their heads down until the reign of Henry's daughter Mary.

The final years

Henry's next marriage, to Anne of Cleves in 1540, was doomed from the start. Anne was a poor choice: she didn't speak English or French, sang like a strangled cat and preferred needlework to a wild night out. More importantly, Henry just didn't fancy her. Luckily for Anne, she escaped with a divorce after just six months.[24] Chief minister Thomas Cromwell got it in the neck (literally, as it turned out) for having picked out Anne as a future bride. Henry sent him to the Tower on trumped-up charges of heresy. Despite sending pleading letters to the king, Cromwell

23. *Aske was hanged in chains in July 1537 outside Clifford's Tower in York, as a gruesome reminder of how the king dealt with rebels.*
24. *The divorce settlement was very generous: Anne got Richmond Palace and Hever Castle, the former family home of the Boleyn family. In fact, Henry and Anne became good friends. She even rode to Queen Mary's coronation alongside the future Elizabeth I.*

was executed in July 1540, on the same day that the king married Catherine Howard, his fifth wife. Cromwell's head was boiled then set upon a spike on London Bridge.

Nineteen-year-old Catherine Howard had caught 49-year-old Henry's eye while he was still married to Anne of Cleves. Foolishly she kept in touch with some of her old sweethearts, buying their silence by giving them posts in the royal household. When Archbishop Cranmer passed on one of her love notes to the king, he went stark raving mad. As you've probably guessed already, the king soon had all of her exes rounded up and, less than two years after their marriage, Catherine was stripped of her title of Queen. On 10 December 1541 her former lovers Thomas Culpeper and Francis Dereham were executed – one beheaded, the other hung, drawn and quartered. Catherine prepared for the worst and even had a chopping block brought to her cell so she could practise looking her best on the big day. Her final words were: 'I die the Queen of England but I would rather have died the wife of Thomas Culpeper.' Take that, Henry!

food, glorious food

The English were known as gluttons in the rest
of Europe, and Henry VIII set the example –
one feast at Greenwich Palace lasted over seven
hours. The 200-strong kitchen staff at
Hampton Court provided meals of up to 14
courses for some 600 people in the Great Hall.
Many dishes were designed to show off the
king's wealth and power. Some were just
bizarre: a 'cockatrice' was made by sewing the
front half of a cockerel onto the back half of a
baby pig! Other dishes included:

- spit-roasted boar • grilled beavers' tails
- whale meat • whole roasted peacock
- tripe – lungs, spleen and even cows' udders
- boar's head • roasted swan • marzipan
- strawberries and cream.

The drinks bill at Hampton Court must have
been astronomical: in just one year, Henry and
his guests quaffed 600,000 gallons (2.7 million
litres) of ale (more than enough to fill an
Olympic-size swimming pool) and around
75,000 gallons (341,000 litres) of wine
(enough to fill 1,500 bathtubs).

However, Henry usually ate in private, with his
own French chef on call 24/7. The king took
his pick from a giant buffet that was freshly
prepared each day. Before he ate, a servant
called a 'sewer' washed the royal hands in
scented water, then dried them.

Hello, big boy

- All that eating was bound to affect Henry's waistline, and after a bad jousting injury in 1536 the lack of exercise made the king even fatter. Late portraits of Henry show a man almost as wide as he was tall – his waist may have been a button-bursting 60 in (152 cm), compared to 35 in (89 cm) as a young man of 23.

- In later life the king needed a staff to help him walk, and by 1545 he was using a wheelchair known as a 'tramme', which was probably pulled along by men heaving on ropes. A form of stairlift was built to help him climb stairs at Whitehall Palace, while another device winched him onto his horse.

- To hide his expanding waistline, Henry began wearing padded clothes with puffy sleeves. Out of respect for the king, everyone at court started wearing padded clothing too.

- Henry's clothing was often decorated with slashing – pieces of silk pulled through cuts in the velvet jacket. This fashion started before Henry's day, when men would come off the battlefield with their clothing ripped. Soon clothes were deliberately slit to achieve the same macho effect.

- A codpiece was basically a cup to cover up a man's private bits. It was worn on the outside of the clothing and decorated with bows and jewels (giving us the term 'family jewels'). It also doubled as a manbag for coins, small weapons and snuff. The ever-vain Henry began padding his codpiece and his court followed suit. Needless to say, codpieces became increasingly oversized. Henry even had an extra-large codpiece built into his suits of armour to intimidate his enemies in battle. When one of these was put on display during the 19th century, it was worn smooth by women touching it for luck!

from monarch to monster

As he grew older, Henry became more beastly by the day:

- He beat Thomas Cromwell around the head and swore at him.

- When he got in a strop, Henry called his minister Thomas Wriothesley 'my pig'.

- As an old man, the king would threaten his entire court by saying 'there was no a head so fine he would not make it fly'.

- Louis Perreau, French ambassador to England during the 1530s, called him 'the most dangerous and cruel man in the world'. Perreau's successor, Charles de Marillac, said that Henry 'does not trust a single man...and he will not cease to dip his hand in blood as long as he mistrusts his people'.

By the 1540s Henry was over the hill, his body horribly bloated and covered in disgusting boils. More foul-tempered than ever, the king was also terrified of dying, so he surrounded himself with a team of doctors and apothecaries (potion makers). Not that any of this stopped the old dog from marrying one last time. Catherine Parr, his sixth and final wife, was more a nurse than anything else. However, she stupidly argued with Henry over religion. Working himself up into a froth, the king ordered her arrest. One story says that once he heard that Catherine had gone to bed crying, Henry cancelled the order.

Henry spent his last few months in a small room while palace life continued as normal. Courtiers bowed to an empty throne and feasts were still held in the great dining hall. Henry's doctors were afraid to tell him that he was dying because the law banned them from predicting the king's death. Finally, on 28 January 1547, the king gasped his last breath, aged 55. It's said that his last words were: 'Monks, monks, monks!' Henry was buried in St George's Chapel in Windsor Castle, next to his wife Jane Seymour.

A big man with a giant personality, Henry VIII was one of a kind. Before Bluff King Hal, the private lives of kings and queens were almost unknown outside the court. But the colourful love life of this handsome rogue was followed in minute detail. He sensationally married four commoners out of love (or lust) in an age when most royal marriages took many years of careful negotiation. If he were alive today he would be followed everywhere by a pack of photographers, waiting hungrily for a glimpse of a new lover or another foul-mouthed outburst.

Love me or loathe me, I'm a tough act to follow.

Going, going, gone

King Henry VIII was horrified by disease, and he spent every summer moving around the south of England to avoid the dreaded sweating sickness (known in Europe as 'the king of England's disease'). This didn't stop him coming down with one health problem after another:[25]

Age 22: Catches smallpox but not scarred by it.

Age 33: First attack of malaria, which plagues him for the rest of his life.

Mid-30s: Nearly drowns after falling headfirst into a muddy ditch while out hunting. He is saved by a quick-thinking footman.

Age 35: A jousting accident leads to ulcers on both legs. In the king's later years, the pain was so severe that he often cried out in agony. The treatment was just as horrific: the ulcers were regularly cut into and dressed with an ointment that contained lead. This poisoned Henry's blood and may have gradually affected his mind.

Age 39: Hurts his left foot playing tennis.

25. It was partly his own fault, as Henry could have looked after himself better. In a toast to John Colet, Dean of Westminster, in 1513, the king held up a glass of wine and said: 'Let every man have his doctor. This is mine.'

Age 44: Another jousting accident knocks the king out for two hours. By now his fits of rage are made worse by lack of sleep, sore throats and terrible headaches.

Age 45: Develops a painful growth on the side of his nose. Due to his diet, Henry is now also suffering from severe diabetes and dropsy, which causes his whole body to swell up.

Age 50: Catches tertian fever. Symptoms include hot and cold flushes and sweaty fits, leading to violent behaviour every other day.

Age 55: Spends the last eight days of his life in bed, surrounded by the awful pong of his bursting leg ulcers.

Dead: Henry's monstrously bloated corpse is said to have exploded two weeks after his death. When the lead casing of his coffin burst, stray dogs wandered into St George's Chapel and licked up the blood that had spilled out (though the same story has been told of other monarchs, so it may be just a myth). Another tale claims that Mary had her father's tomb at Windsor opened and his body removed and burnt.

Execution of Archbishop Cranmer, 1556
Woodcut from Foxe's *Book of Martyrs*, 1563

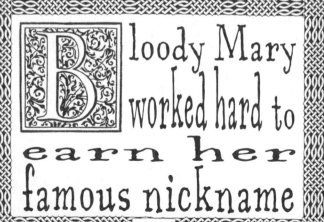

Bloody Mary worked hard to earn her famous nickname

CHAPTER THREE

Bloody Mary, the Godly Imp and the Nine Days' Queen

gly, wicked, cruel, mad, bloody… these are just some of the insults thrown at Mary I, the first ever queen of England. But was she really so much worse than her father, who is thought to have had over 70,000 people put to death during his bloodthirsty reign?

Henry's first child, Mary was born in Greenwich Palace in the small hours of 18 February 1516. Named after her beautiful aunt,[1] she had the flaming red hair of her

---

1. *Henry VIII's younger sister, who was married off to the ageing and decrepit Louis XII of France, and widowed just two months later.*

parents, her father's clear skin, and piercing eyes. If you believe some reports, she was the spit of her dad. Though half-Spanish, Mary was brought up as an English princess. Like most royal children in those days, she didn't live with her parents, but was moved around from palace to palace so her mother Catherine of Aragon could easily pop over for a visit. As a special treat, little Mary went to court for big occasions and festivals such as Christmas.

Bright, precocious Mary was educated from the age of 4 by her governess Margaret Pole, countess of Salisbury. Henry VIII doted on his daughter, calling her his 'pearl of the world'. He loved to carry her around in his arms, showing her off to his courtiers. He once boasted that 'This girl never cries,' and was especially proud of Mary's musical skills. On one visit to court she famously toddled after the organist Dionysius Memo, who had been playing for the king's guests, and demanded that he keep playing. By 7, Mary was also a talented dancer, impressing a Spanish visitor who said 'No woman could do better.'

Bringing up baby

As the daughter of the king and queen of England, baby Mary was fussed over by a large team of carers:

- Her chief nanny was Lady Margaret Bryan, whom her sister Elizabeth called 'Muggie'.

- Dry nurses made sure the nursery ran like clockwork.

- Wet nurse[2] Katherine Pole ensured the princess never went hungry.

- Her ladies-in-waiting included four women who took turns to rock her cradle.

- A laundress washed her clothes (though in Tudor times babies were often kept in the same nappy for several days in a row).

- She had her own dressmaker.

- A spiritual advisor took care of her soul.

- Mary's household staff included cooks, music teachers and maids.

- She also needed her own treasurer. As Mary grew, so did her household: by the time she was 4 her expenses had risen to £1,100 a year (worth about £400,000 today).

2. *A woman hired to breastfeed and care for someone else's child.*

In 1525 Mary was named Princess of Wales by her father. Though just 9 years old, she was given her very own court at Ludlow Castle near the Welsh border. This was effectively the capital of Wales, and Mary had 300 staff working for her. Here, Mary grew from a child into a charming and talented young woman who could speak several languages. She was now taught by Thomas Linacre, a renowned Oxford scholar, though part of every day was also set aside for outdoor fun – Mary loved horses and hunted throughout her life. She even had her own pack of hounds, and birds of prey for hawking.

If all this sounds jolly, in reality Mary was a little girl living in a grown-up world. She was expected to give orders to her staff and win over visitors to court.[3] Not much is known about her childhood friends, though she did have her own jester, Jane Cooper, to entertain her.[4] Young Mary had a tough time in other ways – she was a sickly child with poor eyesight who was plagued by toothache and terrible headaches.

3. In July 1521, aged 5½, she entertained visitors with a performance on the virginals (harpsichord).
4. One of the few women known to have held this job.

If Mary had been a boy, English history would have been very different (if a lot less interesting). As a girl, she was never expected to become queen. Instead, she was used by her father to strike deals with his rivals in France and Spain. Mary always expected to be married off to a foreign prince. Forget love and romance – royal marriage was all about politics and money.

At the age of 2½, her first suitor was another toddler, the heir to the French throne. In 1520, Henry changed tack and tried to fix her up with Emperor Charles V, who was almost old enough to be her father. In 1522 the teenage emperor came to visit and his 6-year-old princess cousin danced and played for him. In the end, Charles decided to marry Isabella of Portugal instead. The suitors kept on coming, and by the time her father died, Mary had seen so many she must have struggled to remember half of them.

In disgrace

Mary's world was turned upside down when Henry VIII dumped her mother, Catherine of Aragon, for Anne Boleyn. Anne really had it in for Mary: she stopped her from seeing her parents, and though Mary wrote to her mother in secret, she never saw her again.[5] The king's new partner saw Mary as a bitter rival, once saying: 'I am her death and she is mine.' She ordered her maids to box the young girl's ears if she was naughty. Things could have been worse, though – Anne might have had her executed.[6]

In return, Mary loathed Anne Boleyn so much she couldn't bear to say her name, calling her 'that woman'. She sided with her mother, Catherine of Aragon, who also had many supporters among the women at court. Stubborn and brave, Mary refused to vanish from public life by entering a convent. As part of his efforts to get a divorce, Henry said that Mary was no longer to be called 'princess', but

5. She did go to Catherine's funeral in 1536.
6. Anne Boleyn paid a fortune teller to prophesy that she could never have Henry's children while Mary or her mother were still alive!

rather 'the Lady Mary'. The 17-year-old Mary stood up to her father and refused to recognise that his marriage to her mother was void (which also made Mary illegitimate).

The king was furious – his word was law and there was no room for argument. In punishment, he sent Mary to Hatfield House, Hertfordshire, in December 1533 to serve as lady-in-waiting to her baby sister Elizabeth, who was Anne Boleyn's daughter. Mary was now in disgrace, effectively banned from court and under house arrest under the watchful eye of Lady Anne Shelton, Anne Boleyn's aunt.

Things went from bad to worse. In 1536, Mary's mother died – and at court, Anne Boleyn reportedly danced for joy. But when she too failed to give the king a son, Thomas Cromwell soon hatched a plan to get rid of her. After Anne's death, Henry offered to pardon Mary if she would acknowledge him as head of the Church of England and agree that she was no longer a rightful heir to the throne. But Mary stuck to her guns.

Mary, Mary, quite contrary

At Hatfield, Mary (now a troublesome teen) did her best to make life a nightmare for everyone. She spent days in her room, weeping non-stop. It was hard having to bow down to her baby sister Elizabeth. Mary objected to calling her 'Princess', and on one occasion refused to step into a carriage after Elizabeth. When a courtier shoved her in, Mary complained to court about this 'act of violence'.

You have to feel sorry for Mary. The change in her father's behaviour must have been incredibly painful, as she had always loved him dearly. When Henry VIII paid a visit to Hatfield in January 1534, he played with Elizabeth while Mary was locked in a room upstairs. As he was leaving, he saw her through the window. Raising his cap in salute, purely out of politeness, he rode off.

What's Elizabeth got that I haven't?

It wasn't long before Henry sent round a group of nobles to twist Mary's arm. The earl of Essex threatened to 'beat her to death, strike her head against the wall until he made it as soft as an apple'. Though Mary still refused to sign,[7] the stress was making her ill. A few days later she caved in and agreed to her father's demands. She regretted this for the rest of her life.

So Henry VIII had, after a fashion, made his peace with Mary, and she quickly became good friends with his new wife Jane Seymour,[8] becoming godmother to Prince Edward, her new brother. Now that the king had his precious son and heir, Mary was given back her own household, including her favourite maid Susan Clarencieux, and was allowed to stay in the royal palaces again.[9]

7. *Thomas Cromwell was at his wits' end: in a letter sent to Mary in June 1536 he called her 'the most obstinate woman that ever was'.*
8. *While Jane was pregnant, Mary sent her cucumbers from her own garden as a gift.*
9. *Mary's favourite residences were Hatfield House in Hertfordshire, the Palace of Beaulieu in Essex (also called New Hall), Richmond Palace in Surrey, and Hunsdon, also in Hertfordshire.*

Mary was given an allowance of £40 per quarter. Though you got a lot for your money in those days, it was very little for a princess, and Mary found it hard to live within her means. Things can't have been that bad, though, as Mary became a fashion queen. She adored clothes and jewels, and during her years of disgrace a number of her finest clothes and jewels had been taken away in punishment. Now back in favour, she spent a fortune on French gowns and velvet and satin from Italy – in December 1537 alone she blew her entire budget on 100 new gowns.

On the surface, Mary was having the time of her life. But the years of struggle had taken their toll. In a portrait of Mary painted in 1544, she seems sad and distant. Mind you, it was never easy living in Henry VIII's shadow, and Mary still had to tiptoe around her father's increasingly bad-tempered and dangerous moods. Many of her supporters had already been executed for treason, including her old governess Margaret Pole, who was hacked to death by a novice axeman in 1541.

Backstabbers, Inc.

Sixteenth-century England was a rough and dangerous place. Henry VIII took 7,000 troops with him when he headed north to Yorkshire. Mary, Edward and Elizabeth rarely left southeast England, afraid of what might happen behind their backs if they left London. Some parts of England were completely beyond their control, such as Tynedale near the border with Scotland. As a result, there were numerous rebellions against the Tudors:

1536: Pilgrimage of Grace
  Ringleader: Robert Aske, a lawyer.
  Cause: Protest against the break with Rome.

1549: Kett's rebellion
  Ringleader: Robert Kett, a Norfolk tanner.
  Cause: Protest against rich landowners who were fencing off common land.

1554: Wyatt's rebellion
  Ringleaders: English nobles Sir Thomas Wyatt the Younger, Sir James Croft and Sir Peter Carew.
  Cause: Protestant uprising against marriage of Mary to Philip II of Spain.

1569: Northern rebellion
  Ringleaders: Charles Neville, 6th earl of Westmorland, and Thomas Percy, 7th earl of Northumberland.
  Cause: Catholic rebellion hoping to replace Elizabeth I with Mary, Queen of Scots.

1570: Ridolfi plot
Ringleader: Roberto di Ridolfi, an Italian banker.
Cause: Planned Catholic invasion to overthrow Elizabeth, backed by Philip II of Spain.

1583: Throckmorton plot
Ringleader: English nobleman Sir Francis Throckmorton.
Cause: Yet another Catholic plot to murder Elizabeth I.

1586: Babington plot
Ringleader: Anthony Babington, a young nobleman.
Cause: Full marks for persistence – another Catholic plot to murder Elizabeth I. This one led to the execution of Mary, Queen of Scots.

1601: Essex's rebellion
Ringleader: Robert Devereux, earl of Essex.
Cause: Half-baked coup d'état against Elizabeth after Essex had fallen out of favour with the queen.

Elizabeth's court also housed its share of foreign spies. The queen had her own network of spies in England and abroad, run by Sir Francis Walsingham. In a famous incident in May 1593, the poet and playwright Christopher Marlowe was killed in a pub brawl in Deptford, south London. A former spy, some people think he may have been bumped off because he knew too much.

Soon after Henry married Catherine Howard in 1540, Mary returned to court. She didn't see eye to eye with the new queen, but Henry's sixth and final wife, Catherine Parr, became a close friend. They shared a love of clothes, jewels, dancing and music, reading and chatting. In 1544 Mary was made an heir to the throne again (second in line after her brother Edward). She was now an important European princess once more, and the hunt for a suitable husband began – and failed – again. Two likely candidates were Dom Luis of Portugal, brother-in-law of Charles V, and Duke Philip of Bavaria, a German prince. Taking Mary on a walk through the bishop of Westminster's gardens in December 1539, bold as brass Philip kissed Mary – something no stranger had ever done before. But the marriage fell through because of wrangles over money.

In many ways, Henry still treated his daughter like a child. When he died in January 1547, Mary wasn't told for several days. But Henry's will confirmed that she was an heir to the throne, and with her father dead, she was free at last – or so she thought…

The 'most precious jewel'

This is probably a good place to take a look at the next king in Mary's life, her little brother Edward.[10] He entered the world on Friday 12 October 1537 at Hampton Court, ending his father's anxious 27-year wait for a son. Given all the blood, sweat and tears it had taken to produce an heir, you can understand why Henry was paranoid about his son's health. At Edward's baptism three days later, anyone coming from areas affected by the plague was banned from court. Nonetheless, a grand ceremony celebrated his arrival, with a huge procession along the galleries to the royal chapel. Baby Edward was wrapped in a magnificent fur-lined robe and carried under a canopy held by four of the king's ministers.

Just 12 days later, Edward's mother Jane Seymour died, probably from an infection caused by poor hygiene (though spiteful rumours at the time whispered that cruel Henry had ordered a Caesarean section –

10. *Edward was named after his royal ancestor, Edward the Confessor (1003–1066), one of the last Anglo-Saxon kings of England.*

nearly always fatal at this period – to make sure no harm came to his precious son during the birth).

For the first six years of his life, Edward was surrounded by women. His chief nurse, Margaret, Lady Bryan, had already brought up his elder sisters. She was very bossy and even Thomas Cromwell, the king's chief minister, was scared of her. When she complained how bare Edward's nursery was, Cromwell hastily transferred £5,000 (worth £1.5 million in today's money) into his funds.

It is often said that Edward VI was a sickly child, but the prince was a healthy baby and by all accounts a happy child until the last six months of his life. He was considered a cute little chap, with grey eyes, lily-white skin and fair hair. When he was struck with 'quartan fever', a form of malaria, at the age of 4, Henry went into panic and summoned the finest doctors in the kingdom. They predicted the worst even after Edward, fed up with being poked and prodded, told them to leave him alone.

Health freak

Henry VIII was obsessed with Edward, calling him the country's 'most precious jewel'. He did everything in his power to shield his son and heir from disease:

- Nobody under the rank of knight was allowed to visit the young prince.

- Edward's rooms were washed down three times a day to keep them free of disease.

- Henry personally vetted all of Edward's servants and no-one could touch the prince unless they had the king's permission.

- All Edward's foods were tasted for poison, all his clothes were examined and then perfumed, and an extra kitchen and washhouse were built at Hampton Court to keep up with all the extra work.

- Even servants who brought in firewood were checked for disease.

You can't be too careful, can you?

Not everyone in England wished the young prince good health. The enemies of the king even turned to black magic – dolls were found with pins stuck into them. Thomas Cromwell's spies also heard nasty rumours doing the rounds that baby Edward was a born murderer. Though this sounds far-fetched, in those days there was a strong belief in magic, and evil gossip quickly became fact. We can only guess how seriously the court took this threat, though it's interesting to note that among Edward's own toys was a box filled with sorcerers' tools, while another contained 'dried dragon', probably some sort of herb.

When you consider how long Henry waited for a son, it's odd that he visited him so rarely. In fact, Edward got more attention from his sisters Mary[11] and Elizabeth. Edward also became fond of Henry's new wife Catherine Parr, calling her his 'most dear mother'. Though the young prince led a carefree life as a child, playing cards and dancing with his friends,[12] he wasn't always well behaved.

11. 'I love you most,' he wrote to her in 1546.
12. His childhood sweetheart was Jane Dormer, 'my Jane', later duchess of Feria.

Like father, like son

Like his father, Edward was horribly spoilt. Nothing was too grand for the future king: rooms hung with expensive tapestries, gold and silver plates and cups, clothes and books encrusted with precious stones and gold. Even as a young boy, Edward owned many animals, including a pack of hounds and fighting bears, and in one (questionable) portrait, aged 6, he is shown holding a monkey that may have belonged to the court fool, Will Somers.

During one visit by foreign ambassadors, he buried his face in his nurse's shoulder and refused to let them kiss him. Like his father, Edward had a ferocious temper. He once ripped all the feathers off his pet falcon.

Henry had big plans for his son. His own father had spent many years battling to have the Tudor dynasty recognised by the rest of Europe, and he was determined to ensure its survival. When Edward's marriage to the Scots princess Mary[13] was rejected in 1542, Henry launched a savage campaign of terror, later known as the 'Rough Wooing'.

13. *We shall meet her again in Chapter 4 as Mary, Queen of Scots.*

By now Edward was back at Hampton Court, where he was groomed for greatness by a team of scholars. A born swot, he spoke Latin and French fluently and later wrote secret messages to himself in ancient Greek to hide his thoughts from nosy courtiers; over a hundred of his essays still survive. Henry arranged for the sons of lords to be taught alongside the future king, and doodles of schoolmates can still be seen on Edward's schoolwork. One such boy, Barnaby Fitzpatrick, became a close and lasting friend. In some accounts, Barnaby was Edward's whipping boy,[14] but this seems unlikely as we know that the prince himself was occasionally beaten by his tutors.

A chip off the old block, Edward was fascinated by war; portraits show him wearing a jewelled dagger of gold hanging from a rope of pearls. In 1550 the 12-year-old prince started to keep a daily journal, or chronicle, and he clearly got very excited about his father's campaigns in Scotland and France.

14. See page 35. In theory, if the whipping boy was the prince's friend it would stop Edward from misbehaving.

Yet the young prince was blissfully unaware of the danger closer to home as his father Henry grew weaker. Even as the king lay dying, Edward Seymour, earl of Hertford, and Sir William Paget were already planning how to take control of the boy. When Henry died on 28 January 1547, Seymour hopped on his horse and whisked Prince Edward to the Tower of London. Three days later, Seymour was made Lord Protector – which meant he would rule the country on the boy king's behalf – while Paget would be First Minister. Only then was Henry VIII's death made public and Edward VI proclaimed king.

There followed a greedy scramble to grab titles and grants of land, and Seymour made himself duke of Somerset. He was now the most powerful man in England.[15] Along with the title came an income of 8,000 marks[16] a year (worth £1.6 million today), more than double the amount given to Princesses Mary and Elizabeth.

15. He was also Jane Seymour's brother and therefore Edward's uncle.
16. A mark was worth £⅔, or 13 shillings and 4 pence.

The boy king

Though his reign started full of hope, Edward was at the mercy of some very powerful and ruthless men. They were determined to hang on to the wealth snatched by Henry VIII from the monasteries. Somerset's greatest rival was his jealous younger brother Thomas Seymour, who, as King Edward's uncle, demanded a greater share of power. Somerset attempted to buy off his brother with titles, but Seymour always wanted more. He sneakily began smuggling pocket money to King Edward, urging him to rule on his own.

When Edward ignored this advice, Seymour went to Plan B and secretly married Henry VIII's widow Catherine Parr, whose household included the 13-year-old Princess Elizabeth. Thomas's plans to marry Elizabeth suffered a setback when his wife found them kissing. But when Catherine died a few months later, Seymour began pestering the young princess by letter. By now he was openly asking other nobles to support a rebellion. Remarkably, though everyone knew what he was up to, he wasn't arrested.

Then, on 16 January 1549, Seymour went one step too far. He had forged the keys to Edward's rooms at Hampton Court and, in the middle of the night, decided to kidnap the king. Entering through the garden, he crept into the royal apartment. Not quietly enough, however – he woke up Edward's pet spaniel, who began to bark. In a fright, Seymour shot the dog. When the royal guards rushed to the scene and demanded an explanation, Seymour fibbed that he was just testing them!

No-one believed him. On 20 March, Seymour was executed at the Tower of London – just the latest in a series of disasters during Somerset's rule as Lord Protector. Somerset's forces won a crushing victory against the Scots at the Battle of Pinkie Cleugh in September 1547, but the cost of the war was huge. When the French attacked English troops in Boulogne in August 1549, he was forced to withdraw from Scotland. It was only a matter of time before he too would fall from power.

The crown faced financial ruin. From April 1549 a series of riots and rebellions broke out across the country. Though they were soon stamped out, the Privy Council (the king's official advisors) decided it was time for Somerset to go. In a panic, Somerset kidnapped the king and sped to Windsor Castle, where poor Edward wrote: 'Methinks I am in prison.'[17] But this was the last act of a desperate man and Somerset soon found himself in the Tower. Two years later, in January 1552, his head parted company with his shoulders.

John Dudley, duke of Northumberland, now had even more control over Edward, as he packed the Privy Council with his own supporters. By now, Edward had strong Protestant beliefs – he was often seen taking notes during sermons – prompting one unkind writer to call him a 'godly imp'. He especially looked up to Thomas Cranmer, archbishop of Canterbury, who wanted to reform the English Church. Always watching in the shadows, Northumberland took advantage of Edward's beliefs to increase his own power.

17. *Edward was already living like a prisoner, as security at the palace was so strict. Even the cushions he sat on had to be tested for possible dangers, and he couldn't go for a walk until the guards had made a thorough search of the park.*

Edward clashed with his elder sister Mary, who continued to celebrate the Catholic Mass in her private chapel. When she visited her 13-year-old brother at court, they argued so fiercely they both burst into tears. It didn't help that Mary was old enough to be his mother and she often treated Edward like a child. She had already been bullied by her father and this time she wasn't giving in.

In June 1550, Mary even hatched a plan to escape to the Netherlands, helped by her cousin Charles V. But when three of the emperor's ships arrived off the coast of Essex, she backed out at the last minute. Luckily for her, the whole episode was quietly forgotten and she spent Christmas at court – the last time Henry's three children were together.

Bear-baiting was a favourite pastime of Edward VI.

Wedding vows

Today's wedding service dates from the time of Edward VI, and still includes original phrases such as 'to love, cherish and obey' and 'for better or worse, for richer or poorer, in sickness and in health'. Edward's service also ruled that wedding rings were to be worn on the third finger of the left hand. This went back to an ancient Egyptian tradition that this finger was directly connected to the heart by the 'vein of love'.

Edward wasn't only interested in religion – by now his lessons included riding, jousting, hunting and tennis. He wore the finest clothes, including a cape covered in diamonds, and he enjoyed watching the so-called sport of bear-baiting. But he was determined to finish the work his father Henry had started, looting the churches to fill his own treasuries. Other reforms went deeper: he made English compulsory in all church services,[18] banned music and art in churches, and had many

18. *Archbishop Cranmer's* Book of Common Prayer *is still the basis for services in the Church of England.*

saints' tombs demolished. In Oxford, a huge chunk of the university library was torched in giant bonfires.

Edward's reforms might have gone further, but it became clear in spring 1553 that he was not long for this world. Aged just 15, he was sick with the lung disease called 'consumption' (tuberculosis). Yet again, the vultures were circling. It's said that the heartless duke of Northumberland hired a witch to give Edward a potion containing arsenic, a poison; this kept the king alive, but in terrible agony. Northumberland wanted to keep Edward VI alive as long as possible. He hoped to persuade the king to change his will so that Lady Jane Grey, a Protestant (who also happened to be Northumberland's daughter-in-law), would become the next queen.

Edward had probably already made up his mind about who should succeed him, knowing that if his Catholic sister Mary became queen, she would undo all his reforms. Edward VI died on 6 July 1553. His last words were: 'I am faint; Lord have mercy upon me and take my spirit.'

God help us from doctors

In a last-ditch effort to save Edward VI, his doctors gave him a concoction of spearmint, turnip, dates, raisins, celery, and pork from a 9-day-old piglet. It didn't work.

Bleeding was a popular treatment for many ailments. The Tudors believed that too much blood was bad for the body. Blood-sucking leeches were used to drain the blood away. Other cures could be quite imaginative:

- **Asthma:** Swallow young frogs.

- **Smallpox:** Hang red curtains around your bed and the red light will cure you.

- **Aching joints:** Wear the skin of a donkey.

No wonder Edward's minister William Cecil once said: 'God help us from doctors.' You won't be surprised to hear that few people in Tudor England lived beyond their 40th birthday.

Leeches

The queen who never was

As the king lay dying, the duke of Northumberland was already busy greasing the palms of the Privy Council, promising lavish grants of land when Lady Jane Grey became queen. He also persuaded them to keep quiet about Edward's death until Lady Jane had safely been moved to London.

Lady Jane was the great-granddaughter of Henry VII, and at one stage our old friend Thomas Seymour had planned to marry her off to her cousin Edward VI. Though Seymour got the chop, Lady Jane was still very much a feature at the royal court, especially after her father was created duke of Suffolk in October 1551. Jane was no stranger to court intrigue – she had joined Lady Elizabeth in the household of Catherine Parr and Thomas Seymour – but the poor girl almost fainted from shock when she first heard of Northumberland's plan to make her queen.

What became of Edward?

Edward's funeral did not take place for four weeks – he was all but forgotten in the tussle between Lady Jane Grey and Mary. An argument over whether he should be buried according to Protestant or Catholic traditions added to the delay. In the meantime, his body was sealed inside a coffin lined with a thin sheet of lead. This could be soldered shut to prevent nasty rotting smells from escaping. At least he fared better than Anne Boleyn, whose remains were crammed into an old arrow chest and her head thrown in on top. A myth lingers on that a substitute corpse is buried in Westminster Abbey while the real body of Edward VI is somewhere in the grounds of Greenwich Palace.

Lady Jane was proclaimed queen on 10 July 1553, just four days after Edward's death. Many had barely heard of her, so she got a lukewarm reception. A young barman, Gilbert Porter, cried out that Mary was the rightful queen. He was promptly arrested and had his ears cut off for this bold remark.[19] Hearing the news, Mary fled to Norfolk, where she had the support of the local nobles – a big gamble

19. He was later made into a hero by Mary's supporters.

for these men who were putting their lives on the line by backing her cause. Many ordinary people also supported Mary, believing she was the true queen.

Slowly the tide turned in Mary's favour. When Northumberland left London to confront Mary's forces, his supporters melted away. Though Londoners were offered tenpence a day to fight for Lady Jane, there were few takers. Meanwhile Mary rode out to meet her army in person on a splendid white horse. Boldly she stated her claim and even put a price on Northumberland's head: £1,000 in lands, dead or alive! Lady Jane, already signing herself 'Jane the Quene,' was persuaded by her father to give up the crown (the stress had given him fainting fits). When Mary entered London on 3 August at the head of 10,000 men, she was met by cheering crowds.

The figure of nine days is often trotted out, but Lady Jane's reign lasted about two weeks if you count it from the date of Edward's death. She and her father were duly sent to the Tower. On the way, their carriage was bombarded with rocks and cries of 'Traitor!' Jane's father, the duke of Suffolk, was pardoned,[20] but she and her husband Lord Guilford Dudley were tried, sentenced to death and beheaded in February 1554. After she was blindfolded, she couldn't find the block and stood there whimpering, 'What shall I do, where is it?' until a bystander led her by the arm. The axe swung and Jane's adventure was over. She was just 17.

The duke of Northumberland had already been beheaded, but Mary was merciful towards many others who had stood against her – she realised she needed their support.

As a mark of respect, Lady Jane was executed in private in the grounds of the Tower of London – straight after the public beheading of her husband.

20. Though he was executed 11 days after his daughter for his part in Thomas Wyatt's rebellion (see page 121).

The crown jewels

In her short reign, Lady Jane got a chance to look at the Tudor crown jewels and even got into a fight with her husband over what crown he would wear! The main pieces were:

- Crown of St Edward the Confessor

- State crown of Henry VII

- State sword

- Sceptre: a golden staff held in the left hand to show the monarch's authority

- Orb: a golden ball held in the right hand. It was topped by a cross, to remind the monarch that God's power is greater than theirs.

Most of the Tudor crown jewels were sold off or melted down after the execution of King Charles I in 1649. Just a few have survived and are now part of the present set of Crown Jewels:

- St Edward the Confessor's sapphire, from a ring he once wore

- The central red ruby from the crown Richard III wore at the Battle of Bosworth, also used to crown Henry VII after his victory

- Pearls worn by Elizabeth I

- Ampulla (a flask in the shape of a golden eagle) and spoon, still used to anoint the head of a new monarch with oil.

Bloody Mary

On 19 July 1553, Mary finally became queen of England. After years of being pushed around by her father and brother, Mary knew what she wanted – a Catholic England – and nobody was going to stand in her way. The Privy Council weren't used to being told what to do by a woman, but Mary had a forceful personality – and a vicious tongue at times.[21] On one occasion she reduced Sir William Paget to tears. In the royal household she surrounded herself with loyal supporters, many of them women.

Mary wanted her coronation to be a knock-out – but unfortunately her crown was so heavy she had to use her hands to stop her head from drooping. As she passed through the streets of London, different groups of tradesmen competed to put on the best display. There were spectacular fountains and dragons, and rivers of wine ran down some streets, but the winner was undoubtedly a Dutch acrobat named Peter, who stood on top

21. *While Henry VIII spoke in a surprisingly high-pitched squeak for such a big chap, Mary's voice was probably deeper than her father's.*

of the spire of St Paul's Cathedral holding a giant streamer.[22]

Now it was down to business. Mary was already writing in secret to the Pope and using her influence with Charles V, whom she met privately within a few months of coming to power. At first, Mary returned to Catholic ways in small steps: she brought back many saints' days, a popular move as they were a great excuse for fairs and festivals. But when Mary invited her cousin Cardinal Reginald Pole to come to England to help her run the country, her true intentions were clear.

Now Mary was queen, she had no choice but to find a husband. Three English contenders and several foreigners were put forward, but she plumped for Philip II of Spain, the son of Charles V. Just two weeks after Mary was crowned, the Spanish ambassador offered her Philip's hand in marriage. Philip was already notorious for torturing and burning Protestants, and many of her ministers feared that he would meddle in English affairs.

22. *He was paid the princely sum of £4,000 in today's money for this stunt.*

Though Mary eventually persuaded the court to agree to the wedding, most people in England hated foreigners, and especially the Spanish. When the Spanish embassy rode into London, boys pelted them with snowballs. Within days, Protestants all over the country were up in arms, led by Sir Thomas Wyatt and other nobles, who planned to put Mary's sister Elizabeth on the throne.

Tough as ever, Mary made a stirring speech before the great men of London, asking her citizens to fight for her. Luckily for her, the rebels were spread out over a large area. Wyatt's forces found the city gates blocking their way on 3 February 1554, and after a few skirmishes the rebellion quickly fizzled out. This time there was no merciful Mary: the rebels were hunted down and executed in batches all over London, including Wyatt, whose body was cut into quarters then nailed to the city gates.[23] Mary's sister Elizabeth, linked to the rebellion, was taken to the Tower. Though she was later released, Mary realised her half-sister was not be trusted.

23. Though Mary took pity on Wyatt's wife and children and gave them a yearly grant of money.

Shock horror! When Mary married Philip II, **a Spaniard** became king of England

The famous drink

The name 'Bloody Mary' is linked to several historical figures, but particularly Queen Mary I. However, the famous cocktail was probably invented in the 1920s by American bartender Fernand Petiot at Harry's New York Bar in Paris, when he added spices and Worcestershire sauce to the already popular combination of vodka and tomato juice. When he returned to the US, 'One of the boys suggested we call the drink Bloody Mary because it reminded him of the Bucket of Blood Club in Chicago, and a girl there named Mary.' Others say Petiot named it after his favourite Hollywood star, Mary Pickford.

Despite the rebellion, Mary married Philip of Spain on 25 July 1554. Eleven years younger than Mary, he was probably more interested in getting his hands on the English crown than on Mary. As far as we know, he only ever learned one phrase in English – 'Goodnight, my lords all!' – but he was attentive and caring, and Mary fell for him.[24] She was desperate for an heir, to stop Protestant Elizabeth undoing all her good work after she died.

24. Some say Mary was smitten before ever meeting Philip, after seeing a full-length portrait of him by the famous painter Titian (now in the Prado museum in Madrid, Spain).

Just two months later, Mary sent a joyful message to the Pope saying that she had felt a child growing inside her. Nine months later, no baby had arrived. Philip decided to head to Flanders to fight the French. A distraught Mary watched in floods of tears as his boat sailed off into the sunset. She even got her cook to send tasty pies over to Flanders to win him back, but to no avail.

Abandoned by her husband, Mary set her mind to making England Catholic again – by any means. It took several years to overturn the Protestant laws passed by Henry and Edward, and to make her point she also had some 290 people executed for not being Catholic. Most were burnt at the stake – a particularly gruesome death. While some were famous Church leaders, such as Archbishop Cranmer, most were ordinary young people who had grown up with the new religion.

The queen, now known as 'Bloody' Mary, was widely hated. Over 800 rich Protestants simply left the country, and a dead dog with its ears cut off was thrown through the window of a royal palace in protest. Things only got worse when a costly war with France led to the loss of Calais, England's last toehold in Europe.[25] Mary's popularity wasn't helped by the weather. September 1555 saw the 'greatest rains and floods ever seen in England', followed by poor harvests, starvation and disease. In 1558 England suffered the worst outbreak of plague since the Black Death.

Still heartbroken at Philip's disappearing trick (the war had brought him back to England for just two months), Mary was further humiliated when another baby, due in June, still hadn't arrived in August. Many people were now laughing behind the Queen's back. Mary's 'baby bump' may have been caused by a deadly cancer. We will never know, but Mary finally died, aged 42, on 17 November 1558, probably from the sweating sickness.[26]

25. To show how much this meant to her, Mary supposedly said that when she died, the words 'Philip' and 'Calais' would be found written on her heart.
26. When he learned of her death, her loving husband said: 'I'm reasonably sorry.'

Off with their heads!

A public execution was a fun day out for all the family – people queued through the night to get the best places. Pie sellers and ale merchants did a roaring trade, and cartloads of cherries were sold to crowds watching the burning of Christopher Wade in 1555. Each crime had its own gruesome form of execution:

- **Hanging,** for witchcraft. The victim was usually placed beneath the gallows on a cart pulled by a horse. Once the noose was in place, the horse was led away and the person left to hang. They died slowly and painfully, unless friends and relatives were allowed to pull on the victim's legs to speed up the process.

- **Beheading,** for naughty nobles, was often carried out within the walls of the Tower of London. For Anne Boleyn, a specialist swordsman was brought from France to ensure a quick death. Executioners held up the severed head by the hair, partly to show the crowd, but also so that the head could see its own headless body, as the victim's brain kept working for several seconds after beheading.

- **Burning at the stake,** for heretics (religious dissidents). Friends were sometimes allowed to hang gunpowder around the victim's neck to bring a quick end. But damp, green wood was used to burn Protestant martyr Nicholas Ridley in 1555 so as to prolong the agony, while in 1538 John Lambert's body was lifted on and off the flames on pikes to increase his suffering.

- **Hanging, drawing and quartering,** for traitors. The prisoner was dragged to the place of execution. There, they were hanged in the normal way but cut down while still alive. The guts and heart were then removed and burnt in front of the victim. The other organs were torn out and finally the head was cut off and the body chopped into four quarters. The pieces were boiled to prevent them rotting too quickly and nailed to the city gates as a grim warning to all. In a fury, Elizabeth once asked Lord Burghley and Sir Francis Walsingham to think of an even nastier death penalty – but they couldn't!

- **Boiling alive,** for poisoners. In the reign of Henry VIII, the bishop of Rochester upset his cook one day. So the cook put a special herb in the bishop's meal that night to give his guests diarrhoea. Unfortunately, two guests died. King Henry ordered that the cook be boiled alive, which became the set punishment for poisoners for the next five years.

Mary's coronation ring was taken to Elizabeth as proof of her death. Elizabeth gave her half-sister a suitably grand funeral, and Mary was buried in Westminster Abbey.[27] But Elizabeth's historians were less forgiving, and once Mary was dead, the knives came out.

Four hundred and fifty years later, the queen is still best known as Bloody Mary. But there was more to Mary than frying Protestants alive. You have to admire her determination, and it's often forgotten that she built up England's bridges, roads and navy. Her court was home to great artists such as the composer Thomas Tallis, and she did much to boost English trade by supporting Richard Chancellor's expedition to Russia. Mary reigned only five years; had she lived another ten or more, her plans to make England Catholic again might have succeeded. If they had, we might be talking about 'Bloody Henry' instead.

27. During the reign of Elizabeth, her tomb became buried under piles of stones from broken altars. When Elizabeth herself died, James I built a magnificent tomb for both sisters.

Will the real Mary step forward?

- **Health freak?** The queen walked 2–3 miles (3–5 km) most days, and loved to ride and hunt.

- **Gambler?** At night Mary loved to bet on cards and dice. At one stage she was blowing nearly a third of her income on gambling.

- **Sweet tooth?** Mary's favourite hard candy, *Manus Christi* ('Hand of Christ'), was made from white sugar, rosewater and powder of pearls, and decorated with gold leaf.

- **Animal lover?** Mary was given a parrot as a pet in 1537, and also had a pet spaniel.

- **Charity worker?** Queen Mary was very generous: she gave 40 shillings to the poor to celebrate the birth of her brother. It was believed in some parts of Europe that the royal touch was divine and could perform miracles, and Mary took very seriously her ability to cure the disease scrofula (known as the 'King's evil').

- **Gift-giver?** Once Edward was born and there was less rivalry between the two sisters, Mary grew very fond of Elizabeth and gave her jewellery and money for dresses. A whizz with a needle, she also made cushions for members of court at Christmas.

I taught those Spaniards a thing or two, didn't I?

In Elizabethan times England learned to punch above its weight

CHAPTER FOUR

Good Queen Bess

he second daughter of Henry VIII, Elizabeth Tudor was born on 7 September 1533 at Greenwich Palace. She had her father's fair skin and long nose, and the dark eyes of her mother Anne Boleyn. Her birth sent Henry into a spin. Astrologers and doctors had been telling him for months he was going to have a son, so Elizabeth's arrival was something of a slap in the face. Though the new princess was given a lavish christening, the mood was low-key – Henry didn't bother to turn up and the usual festive parties and tournaments were cancelled.

At first, little Bess lived in a special nursery built for her at Greenwich. She was doted on by her mother, Anne Boleyn, who dressed her in yellow and green silks that suited her flaming red hair.[1] Even Henry came around. As the king grew bored with Anne, however, his interest in Elizabeth evaporated. The little princess was just 2 years old when her mother was beheaded and branded a witch. As far as we know, Elizabeth rarely spoke about Anne again, and we can only guess what she thought of her father.

At this time, Elizabeth was living in the remote manor of Hunsdon in Hertfordshire, far from court. Now called 'Lady' rather than 'Princess', she was brought up by a team of nannies and tutors. After her mother died, the supply of dresses soon dried up and her chief nanny, Lady Bryan, wrote to Secretary Thomas Cromwell complaining that Elizabeth had no clothes.

1. Green and yellow were also royal colours.

A follower of fashion

- Queen Bess's love affair with clothes began at an early age. On her death, it's said she owned 3,000 dresses and 200 cloaks. In public, she dressed to impress and her clothes were decorated with jewels and embroidered with gold thread. The big ruff worn around the neck by the queen and her courtiers showed their wealth and importance. Some ruffs were so wide that ladies couldn't reach their mouths with a spoon.

- White and black were her favourite colours – a reminder to all that she was the Virgin Queen.

- A typical outfit consisted of: a chemise (vest or undershirt), a stomacher (corset stiffened with wood or iron, used to make her stomach look as small as possible), a petticoat, a farthingale (hooped skirt), stockings, gown, girdle (cloth belt), sleeves, a neck ruff and wrist ruffs. No wonder it took two hours for Elizabeth's maids to dress her!

- To complete the look, the Queen wore accessories such as a fan, a pomander (perfume ball) to ward off foul smells (and possibly infection), earrings, a diamond or pearl necklace and a brooch. As was the fashion, she often wore a miniature prayer book attached to her girdle.

- The queen had a new pair of shoes every week. On the first Christmas of her reign she was given elegant silk stockings by Robert Dudley; she never wore wool stockings again.

- Outdoors, the queen wore rich velvet cloaks, gloves of cloth or leather, and, on a hot day, a hat to shield her pale face from the sun.

- Elizabeth encouraged her courtiers to dress well, and passed laws telling her people what they could and couldn't wear. Woollen hats, for instance, had to be worn on a Sunday. This measure was introduced to help the English wool industry.

- In her youth, Elizabeth wore little make-up, but following an attack of smallpox in 1562, she plastered it on to cover up the scars left on her face. Her face was painted with ceruse, a mix of white lead and vinegar. She also put rouge on her lips and painted her cheeks with red dye.

- The queen was the ultimate fashion victim: she probably died from blood poisoning caused by the lead in her ceruse make-up!

You don't get to look this good without trying.

For once, Henry wasn't being deliberately cruel: he was probably just obsessed by his new wife, Jane Seymour. Luckily, Jane was a kind woman who treated Elizabeth well. More importantly, she gave Henry a son, Edward. The king was now ready to play happy families again. While Mary was made godmother to her brother, 4-year-old Elizabeth carried his christening robe. It was so heavy, she had to be carried herself by a courtier!

Edward's arrival meant the loss of her beloved nanny Lady Bryan. But Elizabeth's new governness, Catherine Champernowne, known as Kat Ashley, was loving, well-educated and utterly devoted to her charge. Elizabeth blossomed. When one of Henry's ministers, Thomas Wriothesley,[2] met the 6-year-old Elizabeth, he was blown away by her confidence and predicted great things for the little girl.

2. Pronounced 'Rizley'.

Magic and superstition

- Tudor England was home to many 'wise' men and women, who helped people with life's problems. Charms were believed to ward off evil or make money, while magic spells were bought in the hope that they might put the kids to sleep or put out fires.

- Henry VII dabbled in alchemy, an early sort of chemistry which tried to turn ordinary metals such as lead into gold (now known to be an impossible task).

- Elizabeth I asked magician and alchemist Dr John Dee to pick a lucky date for her coronation. When he later ran into financial problems, she told him to solve them himself, since he was an alchemist (see above)!

- In 1577 a wax doll of the queen was found with a pin stuck through the heart; it was believed that witches did this to hurt their enemies. Dr Dee was called in to undo the bad magic.

- Because of such beliefs, witches were genuinely feared. Around 100,000 people, mostly women, were executed in 16th- and 17th-century Europe. Suspected witches were often thrown into the water to see if they sank or floated. If they floated, they were found guilty and executed. If they sank, they were innocent – but probably died from drowning!

- King Henry VIII liked to think that Anne Boleyn's witchcraft had tricked him into marrying her, so in 1542 he banned witchcraft if it was used to discover treasure, hurt people, or make them fall in love! In 1569, Elizabeth I passed another law banning the use of magic to cure people, summon evil spirits or find lost possessions. These acts led to vicious witch hunts.

- Most people in troubled Tudor times were highly superstitious and wouldn't travel on certain 'evil' days. Even the level-headed Henry VII was supposedly buried with a piece of St George's leg bone to bring him good luck in the afterlife. He also owned a serpent's tongue on a chain to protect him from sudden poisoning and illnesses. Henry VIII's minister Cardinal Wolsey was said to own a magic ring and have a demon at his command.

- Elizabeth kept a 'unicorn horn' in her cabinet of curiosities, which was thought to ward off illness. It was actually a narwhal tusk brought back by Arctic explorer Martin Frobisher on his return from northern Canada in 1577.

- Many believed that curses had real power. As they grew tired of Henry's rule, the curses flew: people wished 'a turd for the king', even though such talk could have them executed. Elizabeth was charmingly referred to as a 'pisskitchen'.

In 1544 Elizabeth joined her brother in the classroom. As a result, she was taught by famous scholars such as William Grindal and Roger Ascham. From an early age it was clear that she was a gifted student. Like her sister, Elizabeth had a flair for languages. She was also coached in public speaking – unusual for women in those days. Elizabeth learned how to win over a crowd, a powerful tool that would serve her well in the coming years.

But there was also plenty of time for long walks and hunting. Elizabeth's love of horse riding later gave her ministers the heebie jeebies, as they feared a bad fall could injure or even kill her. Tutor Roger Ascham also introduced Elizabeth to the cockpit, and the princess loved nothing more than watching birds, bears and other animals rip each other to pieces. It probably reminded her of life at court.

The next few years must have been unsettling for Elizabeth as stepmothers came and went. In June 1543 she was invited to meet Catherine Parr, Henry's sixth wife. The new queen appealed to the king's better nature and by 1544 Elizabeth was again recognised as third in line to the throne, after Edward and Mary.[3] Like her elder sister Mary, Elizabeth was now seen as a potential match for royal princes from Denmark to Spain.

The final years of Henry VIII's reign were happy ones for Elizabeth. But the king's death in 1547 led to yet more turmoil in her life. When Lord Somerset broke the news, Elizabeth and her brother Edward both burst into tears. If she had known what lay ahead, she would have wept for herself as well as her father.

Sob!

Elizabeth must have guessed that the coming years would not be plain sailing.

3. *Henry celebrated by commissioning a painting known as* The Family of Henry VIII. *This shows Henry standing proudly next to his three children and Edward's mother, Jane Seymour. You can see it for yourself if you visit Hampton Court palace.*

Elizabeth keeps her head!

Though Henry had granted Elizabeth a generous allowance of £3,000 a year in his will, she was too young to live on her own, so she moved into Catherine Parr's household at Chelsea Palace. Elizabeth continued with her studies, but, like any teenager, books weren't the only things on her mind. When Catherine Parr's new husband Thomas Seymour – a tall hunk with a trendy beard – began flirting with the 14-year-old princess, it was hard to resist him. Though Elizabeth's governess Kat Ashley warned Seymour to back off, he replied: 'I will not leave off, for I mean no evil.'

On one occasion Seymour cheekily entered the princess's bedroom and chopped her nightgown into 100 pieces! Catherine could believe this was innocent fun, but when she discovered them kissing, enough was enough, and Elizabeth was packed off in disgrace. Soon after, Seymour was accused of plotting against his brother, Lord Somerset, and, worse still, of planning to marry Elizabeth.[4]

4. Elizabeth, Kat Ashley and Elizabeth's loyal servant Thomas Parry were all questioned. Apparently Elizabeth still had a crush on Seymour and smiled whenever his name was mentioned.

Elizabeth was lucky to get off with a warning, and she wisely decided to focus on her books in future. When she visited her brother's court four years later, she wore plain black and white to show how much she had changed. A born actress, Elizabeth knew this would win over Edward, who was now a strict Protestant.

Elizabeth again did the sensible thing after Edward's death in 1553. Once the plot to make Lady Jane Grey queen had clearly failed, she rushed to London with a small army to declare her support for Mary (who already had things well under control). At her sister's coronation, she solemnly swore an oath of loyalty to the new queen.

Mary wasn't fooled for a minute, and asked her sister to attend Catholic Mass at the Royal Chapel to prove her support. This was a tricky one. If Elizabeth didn't go, she'd risk making Mary angry. If she did, it would look bad to her Protestant supporters. In the end, Elizabeth elegantly side-stepped the issue, telling Mary she needed to take spiritual advice before making up her mind.

Elizabeth must have been aware that many Protestant nobles were ready to rebel against Mary. One of them, Sir Thomas Wyatt, sent her a letter telling the princess of their plans. Though she probably agreed with them, she was wise not to reply as the plotters were soon rounded up. Mary ordered her sister to come to London to explain herself. Elizabeth knew she was playing a very dangerous game. One wrong move could give Mary an excuse to get rid of her closest rival.

Again Elizabeth tried to play for time, saying that she couldn't come as she had been struck down by a fever (a half-truth, as her kidneys were playing up). When Mary's doctors insisted that she was well enough to travel, Elizabeth had one more trick up her sleeve. She had herself carried to London on a litter,[5] with 100 horsemen in front and behind her, all dressed in scarlet. Elizabeth, meanwhile, was dressed in white, and had the curtains open to let the world see her suffering.

After a few days at Whitehall Palace, Elizabeth was sent to the Tower – not to a

5. A chair or bed carried on two poles.

dark, damp dungeon but to a royal suite with four rooms and dozens of servants.[6] Wise to her half-sister's tricks, Mary had her smuggled upriver in a barge in the dead of night.[7] As you can imagine, Elizabeth was petrified. In one version of the story, after the princess's boat passed through Traitors' Gate, she refused to go any further. As the rain beat down, a very soggy Elizabeth sat shivering on the stairs up to the gate until Kat Ashley finally persuaded her to enter. All very dramatic, but in reality it was low tide, so Elizabeth probably entered over the drawbridge!

Elizabeth had every reason to be nervous – the observant reader will have spotted that most people who entered the Tower soon lost their head. But just before he was executed, the leader of the rebellion, Sir Thomas Wyatt, proclaimed that Elizabeth knew nothing about the plot. As the weeks went by, Mary relented and Elizabeth was sent to Woodstock Manor in Oxfordshire, where she was held for a year.

6. Even so, Elizabeth must have been badly spooked: it was the very place where her mother Anne Boleyn had spent her final days!
7. Mary would not have been amused to hear that some of the guards at the Tower took off their caps, knelt down and cried out 'God save Your Grace' as Elizabeth passed by.

On the outside, things were moving fast. By now Mary was gooey-eyed over Philip of Spain, who persuaded her to go easy on Elizabeth as he hoped to marry her to his ally, the duke of Savoy. When Elizabeth refused, Mary threatened to lock her up again. But Mary's health was failing. Willing to let bygones be bygones, she was prepared to make Elizabeth her heir on two conditions:

1. **Pay off my debts.**

2. **Keep England Catholic.**

Elizabeth agreed, of course (fingers crossed and hope to die), knowing full well she could do what she liked once she was on the throne.

My turn at last – and I'm not taking any nonsense from anyone.

Elizabeth's reign would be portrayed as a new Golden Age.

Queen Elizabeth

On 17 November 1558, after 15 years of uncertainty, her time had come. For the first and only time in English history, the cry rang out: 'The queen is dead, long live the queen!'

The story goes that Princess Elizabeth was sitting under an oak tree at Hatfield House in Hertfordshire when a horseman galloped up with the news that would change her life for ever. Aged 25, she was now queen of England. But where to start? Wars, plagues and religious strife had left the country bankrupt and divided. And thanks to Mary, Elizabeth would have to kick-start the Protestant Church all over again.

From day one, Elizabeth also had to prove herself to the men at court, who believed that as a woman she wasn't up to the job and needed a husband to help her out. Many nobles undoubtedly looked forward to pushing the young queen around. But just four days into her reign she had dismissed many of them and chosen a new, much smaller, Privy Council. Elizabeth 1, Doubters 0.

10 things you didn't know about Elizabeth I

1. She hated eating in public and took most of her meals in her privy chamber.

2. It's said that the Queen would climb on a chair screaming if she saw a mouse!

3. Elizabeth was very proud that she took a bath once a month, 'whether she needed it or no'.

4. In 1596 a flush toilet, named the Ajax, was invented and built for Queen Elizabeth I by her godson, Sir John Harrington. At first she wasn't that impressed, but once she saw it in action, she wanted them in all of her palaces.

5. The queen owned the first wristwatch in England, given to her by Robert Dudley. It was encased in a bracelet.

6. Elizabeth caught smallpox at 29, and survived. She was lucky: Lady Mary Sidney, who nursed the queen, was so pockmarked by the disease that she never showed her face in court again.

7. She loved marzipan and used a sugary solution to keep her breath fresh. Unfortunately, these made her teeth rot.

8. Though she rarely mentioned her mother Anne Boleyn in public, in 1575 Elizabeth had a ring made which contained a picture of both herself and her mother.

9. Scared to death of being assassinated, for the last years of her life Elizabeth carried around a rusty old sword.

10. During Elizabeth's reign, one in four girls born in England were named after the queen.

Elizabeth honours a hero of the realm.

Once this is over I might have a bath.

Arise, Sir Walter.

Elizabeth was crowned queen on Sunday 15 January 1559. The celebrations were sensational – the coronation banquet alone would have cost about £3.5 million today. Like all the Tudors, Elizabeth knew that a good show could win over the people. As she walked along the blue carpet laid out for her journey to Westminster Abbey, there was pandemonium as the crowds rushed forward to cut out pieces as souvenirs. Yet Elizabeth took her time to meet and greet the crowd and was an instant hit.

She hoped to sort out England's religion once and for all. Within a year, Elizabeth had broken with Rome (again) and made herself head of the Church of England.[8] Elizabeth 2, Doubters 0. Over the next few years she also made it law for all services (and Bibles) to be in English, and reintroduced the *Book of Common Prayer* (still in use today). Elizabeth was no hardcore Protestant – she allowed Catholic traditions such as candlesticks and crucifixes – but this didn't stop a rash of Catholic plots against her.

8. *You may wonder how religious leaders were able to switch from Protestant to Catholic and back again. But Tudor people generally accepted that the best way to obey God was to obey the king (or queen).*

The Virgin Queen

- Elizabeth got this nickname because she never married, but she could have filled a palace with royal suitors such as Prince Eric of Sweden and Archduke Charles of Austria.

- The real love of her life was Robert Dudley, earl of Leicester, whom she nicknamed 'Darling Robin' or 'Sir Eyes'. Though he was already married, Dudley and the queen were inseparable. She once jokingly said: 'You are like my little dog; when people see you, they know I am nearby.' But, though rumours spread like wildfire, marriage was impossible after Dudley's first wife, Amy Robsart, broke her neck falling down a flight of stairs – which looked suspiciously like murder.

- Elizabeth loved to be surrounded by handsome young men showering her with presents. She encouraged them to woo her with sweet words or by dancing with her. Outsiders sometimes mistook this flirting for the real thing. Elizabeth moaned: 'I do not know how such a bad opinion has been formed of me. A thousand eyes see all I do.'

- In 1579 Elizabeth, now 46, considered marrying Henry, Duke of Anjou, brother of Charles IX of France, who was 20 years her junior. After two years of negotiation she changed her mind. The jilted duke pulled off the queen's ring and hurled it to the ground.

What a show!

Dashing Dudley was something of a showman. To impress the queen, in the summer of 1575 he threw a fabulous party at his home, Kenilworth Castle. No expense was spared:

- Dudley added new rooms to the castle for the Queen and her entourage. It's said that when Elizabeth complained that she couldn't see the gardens from her bedroom, he had a new garden built overnight under her window. (The gardens at Kenilworth were lavishly restored by English Heritage in 2009.)

- The moat had a floating island upon it, and an actress dressed as the Lady of the Lake sang a song praising Elizabeth as she passed by.

- There was also an artificial dolphin swimming on the moat, with a band of musicians tucked inside.

- All sorts of entertainments were laid on for the Queen, from plays, feasts, dances and fireworks to bear-baitings, hunting and mock battles.

- The party took years to prepare and lasted 19 days, reputedly costing Dudley £1,000 per day (worth £190,000 today). It almost bankrupted him, but it was worth it. The Queen remembered him to her dying day.

Meanwhile, Elizabeth kept everyone guessing about her love life. Ministers dreaded what would happen if she had no heir. In 1566 Parliament refused to hand over any money until she married. Pointing to her coronation ring, Elizabeth replied: 'I have already joined myself in marriage to a husband, namely the kingdom of England. Do not blame me for the miserable lack of children, for every one of you are children of mine.' The matter was never raised again. Elizabeth 3, Doubters 0.

Yet this was the same woman who had had a teenage crush on Thomas Seymour. Elizabeth loved the company of men and knew that flirting was often the easiest way to get things done. She also played hard to get. A visit from the queen was a sure way to get ahead at court. Some ministers gave their homes an extreme makeover, converting them into the shape of the letter E, but even this didn't guarantee a royal visit.

The queen took advantage of her single status to woo Henry, Duke of Anjou, and later his brother Francis, hoping to form an alliance with France against Spain. Nothing came of it, but the love games kept her European rivals guessing. Even her relationship with Dudley had a political angle: it unnerved her ministers, who were convinced that a word from Dudley would turn her against them.

Elizabeth was a smart cookie, but she also valued the advice of ministers such as William Cecil (later Lord Burghley), Sir Nicholas Bacon and Sir Francis Walsingham (her spymaster, who more than anyone kept her in power). It can't have been easy serving under her, however. While the queen was known for her sharp tongue and ferocious temper (she was her father's daughter), she could also drive her ministers nuts by putting off an important decision until the very last moment.

Elizabeth called Parliament only when she had to. Her court was the real centre of power: a place to wow foreign visitors, make friends and influence people.[9] Winning over the queen could bring fame and fortune, but you had to be prepared to splash out on lavish gifts and fancy clothes.

9. It was also a centre for the arts: Shakespeare was just one of many playwrights who were invited to court to put on plays. Like her father, Elizabeth loved music and dancing, and played the virginals and lute.

Temper tantrums

The queen was a control freak and hated being disobeyed. She refused to employ anybody who was ugly – one young man was turned away from court because he had a front tooth missing. Nobody was allowed to sit while she stood, and anyone addressing the queen had to do so on bended knee. And woe betide anyone who crossed her:

- She swore like a sailor, and once spat on the clothes of an unfortunate courtier who had not dressed to her liking.

- No-one ever dared to beat her at cards because she always sulked or lost her temper.

- She punched and kicked her secretary William Davison.

- She threw a slipper at Sir Francis Walsingham and hit him in the face.

- She once sent a letter to the earl of Essex that was so rude and aggressive that he fainted!

- When she got annoyed and no-one else was around, she boxed the ears of her ladies-in-waiting.

- She attacked the new wife of Robert Dudley, Lettice Knollys, and called her the 'she-wolf'.

- When Elizabeth found out that Lady Mary Shelton had got married in secret, she broke Shelton's finger in a flurry of punches.

- In 1579, John Stubbs wrote a book attacking her plans to marry the duke of Anjou. Elizabeth had him arrested, and Stubbs was punished by having his right hand cut off. Apparently he then took off his hat and raised it with his left hand, saying 'God save the Queen' before fainting.

Some do's and don'ts at court

- Breaking wind in public was one of the greatest crimes you could commit. The earl of Oxford let one rip while bowing to swear his loyalty to Elizabeth. He was so embarrassed, he went into voluntary exile for seven years. On his return, the queen welcomed him back, saying, 'My Lord, I had forgot the fart.'

- The great scholar Erasmus advised guests:

  - **Sit not down until you have washed.**
  - **Place your hands neatly on the table...and not around your belly.**
  - **Don't shift your buttocks left and right as if to let off some blast.**

- The men of Henry VIII's court were forbidden to brawl, duel, or appear in public with their mistresses.

- Kissing was more straightforward. In Tudor times, if a businessman met a colleague and his wife he kissed her straight on the lips, even if they had never met before.

- When performing the volta, an energetic dance in which the man lifted his partner into the air, nobles were advised to remove their rapiers so no-one got stabbed in the process.

- Henry VIII had banned plays that mentioned what was going on at court, but Elizabeth loved the theatre and stood up to strict Protestants who wanted to close down the playhouses. Though Shakespeare's company of actors was popular at court, he rarely refers to Elizabeth in his plays. (Her birth is the climax of his play *Henry VIII*, but this was probably written ten years after her death.) Apparently, she liked the character of Falstaff so much, in *Henry IV Part 1*, that she asked Shakespeare to write something that showed the character in love – this is supposed to have inspired his comedy *The Merry Wives of Windsor*.

Elizabethan court dress made few concessions to the shape of the human anatomy.

Blood relations

Though Elizabeth's reign got off to a flying start, there was trouble ahead. Elizabeth's only serious rival for the throne was her cousin Mary, Queen of Scots, who had grown up in Catholic France and had been married to French king Francis II.[10]

Elizabeth and Mary never met.

Mary headed back to Scotland after Francis's death in 1561. Elizabeth tried to hook her up with Robert Dudley (heaven knows what he thought of this arrangement), but Mary only had eyes for Henry Stewart, Lord Darnley.

Unfortunately for Mary, Darnley wanted to be king himself. He was also convinced Mary was having an affair with her Italian secretary, David Rizzio, so he had Rizzio murdered in 1566. Three months later, Darnley himself was dead. Mary didn't mourn him long: soon she was married again, this time to James Hepburn, Earl of Bothwell.

10. *Mary's mother, Marie de Guise, was from a powerful French family. She once turned down a marriage proposal from Henry VIII.*

A Tudor murder mystery

There was definitely something fishy about Lord Darnley's death:

- **Cause of death:** Strangulation.

- **The evidence:** on 10 February 1567 two dead bodies were found in an orchard outside Edinburgh: Darnley and his valet. Darnley was dressed in his nightgown. On the same night, a huge explosion ripped through Darnley's house.

- **Prime suspect:** Darnley was a drunk and bullied Mary, so she may have had a hand in his death.

- **What happened?** We will never know the full story, but it seems likely that the assassins planned to blow Darnley up while he lay in bed recovering from an illness. He escaped by fleeing from his bedroom, only to be murdered when he got outside.

At this point, civil war broke out in Scotland. In June 1567 Protestant rebels arrested Mary and imprisoned her in Loch Leven Castle. She fled to England, hoping that Elizabeth would help her regain the Scottish throne.[11] But the longer she stayed in England, the more she became a threat to Elizabeth. Matters weren't helped in 1570 when the Pope ordered English Catholics to kill Elizabeth. Until then, Elizabeth had left the Catholics alone, but now the gloves were off: anyone caught celebrating Mass was put in prison for a year.

Catholic conspirators flocked to Mary like moths to a flame. Some, such as the duke of Norfolk, fell hopelessly in love with her. Elizabeth didn't want trouble, and for 19 years she kept Mary under house arrest in various castles around England. Time and again, Mary was linked to plots against the queen, and matters finally came to a head in 1586 when Sir Francis Walsingham 'discovered' a letter from Mary backing a plot to assassinate Elizabeth. It was a set-up, engineered by Walsingham to get rid of Mary once and

11. Her baby son, crowned James VI of Scotland in 1567, was raised by Mary's half-brother, the Earl of Moray. In 1603 James succeeded Elizabeth and became James I of England.

for all. Mary was tried and found guilty of treason. At first Elizabeth did not want to sign her cousin's death warrant (some say she secretly wanted to have her assassinated). When she eventually did sign, she ordered it not to be sealed.

For once, the Privy Council dared to bypass the queen, and in February 1587 it had the letter sealed and delivered. Mary was duly beheaded on 8 February at Fotheringhay Castle, Northamptonshire. The first Elizabeth knew about it was when she heard the church bells ringing in celebration. The queen was hopping mad, but she could do nothing.

Catholic Europe was outraged, and the Pope urged Philip of Spain to invade England. Though the English and their powerful Catholic neighbours tangled time and again over the years, the queen had always tried to avoid a long war – she just didn't have the money to pay for it. Though Dudley persuaded her to support the Protestant Huguenots in France, she soon backed down.

If at first you don't succeed...

Poor Mary, Queen of Scots had a very messy end. She paid the executioner a purse of gold to do a good job. She should have got her money back. Whoosh! The axe came swinging down – and missed! Actually it caught the side of her neck, causing Mary to cry out in pain.

Second time lucky? Not quite. Though the axe cut through most of her neck, the headsman still had to hack through the grisly remnants.

To add insult to injury, when the executioner picked up Mary's head to show it to the crowd, he forgot she wore a wig. He was left holding the wig, while the head bounced onto the floor.

Legend has it that Mary's pet dog was hiding in her skirts all along, refusing to be parted from its owner. It finally emerged covered in blood.

Whimper

The Golden Age

Though she tried to avoid war, Elizabeth was happy to look the other way as English sea captains plundered Spanish treasure ships returning from the New World. In the 1570s she did her best to patch things up by giving back some of the stolen loot on at least two occasions, but everyone could see where this game of cat and mouse was heading.

In 1572, Francis Drake boldly pounced on a Spanish treasure fleet and returned home loaded with booty. Five years later, he repeated the trick after raiding several Spanish colonies. For good measure, he then sailed round the world, the first Englishman to do so. On his triumphant return in 1580 Elizabeth knighted Drake, knowing full well that the Spanish ambassador was watching.

The final straw came when English troops were sent to the Netherlands in support of a Protestant rebellion against Philip's brother Ferdinand.[12] While Philip's commanders

12. *Much of the Netherlands was ruled by the Spanish branch of the Habsburg dynasty at this time.*

ummed and aahed about how to invade England, fiendish Sir Francis sailed into Cádiz harbour and destroyed over 30 Spanish ships, a feat he described as 'singeing the King of Spain's beard'.[13] The invasion of England was delayed by a year, but in 1588 a giant fleet of 130 ships, known as the 'Invincible Armada', finally set sail, carrying 19,000 troops and 8,000 sailors.

The smaller, faster English ships outmanoeuvred the lumbering Spanish galleons, but after five days of fighting the Spanish had only lost three ships. The English then sent in eight fireships packed with burning tar and gunpowder. Remembering what had happened at Cádiz, the Spanish panicked. Now scattered to the four winds, the Armada's commanders had little choice but to head for home. They decided to go the safer but longer way back, around the north of Britain. Bad move! Off the coast of Scotland, the Spanish sailed smack into a hurricane. Half the fleet was destroyed, and many of those who were wrecked off Ireland were

13. This phrase means doing enough to delay your enemy, but not enough to cripple them.

hunted down and killed by English forces. Only 67 out of 130 ships made it back home.

There was still a threat from the 18,000-strong invasion force led by the duke of Parma, expected to land at Margate on the east coast. As a woman, Elizabeth wasn't expected to go to war, but she famously roused her troops at Tilbury docks, saying: 'I know I have the body but of a weak and feeble woman, but I have the heart and stomach of a king, and of a king of England too!' Cue big cheers all round.

Victory over the Armada saved England from invasion, but the queen's triumph was tinged with sadness when her beloved Dudley died just four weeks later.[14]

14. A heartbroken Elizabeth kept Dudley's last letter in a chest in her bedroom until the day she died.

Sailors' tales

• **A Cool Head**

The myth: When the Spanish Armada was sighted, Francis Drake was playing bowls on Plymouth Hoe. Playing it cool, he said there was time to finish the match and still defeat the Spanish; he lost the game, but won the battle.

The truth: Drake did play bowls, but he would surely have jumped into action straight away – unless he knew he had to wait for the tide to turn anyway.

• **Bang for Help**

The myth: Sir Francis Drake took a snare drum on his voyage around the world. When he died, the drum was taken to Buckland Abbey in Devon. It was said that if England was ever in danger again, someone should bang on the drum and Drake would return from the grave to defend his country.

The truth: Throughout history people have claimed to have heard the drum beating – such as when World War I broke out in 1914 – but there have been no sightings of Sir Francis himself.

- **Raleigh's Cloak**

The myth: Explorer and all-round scallywag Sir Walter Raleigh gallantly placed his cloak over a puddle in order to save Queen Elizabeth from getting her shoes muddy.

The truth: The story comes from 17th-century historian Thomas Fuller, noted for his love of a good tale, so who knows?

- **Baccy and Spuds**

The myth: Sir Walter Raleigh introduced both tobacco and potatoes to England.

The truth: Potatoes were first brought back to Europe by the Spanish, while Frenchman Jean Nicot (as in *nicotine*) introduced tobacco to France in 1560, and from there it hopped across the Channel. Sir Walter did help to make smoking popular at court.

A royal progress

Elizabeth and her court travelled across southern England and East Anglia on some 25 'progresses' during her reign. These yearly tours were a chance for the queen to be seen in public, though they must have been a nightmare for her security chiefs as she stopped and spoke to anyone and everyone. She also tucked in to local food without having it tasted first for signs of poison.

A typical royal progress travelled about 10 miles (16 km) a day. There were few good roads, and in bad weather coaches and wagons soon got stuck in the mud. The queen stayed at the houses of nobles along the way. Though this was a great honour, it was also a potential minefield for the host, who had to indulge the monarch without appearing too flash. Elizabeth expected the finest rooms, lavish gifts of jewellery or clothes, and a full line-up of entertainments. When she arrived, everything had to be just so:

- fresh plaster on houses
- flags and tapestries hanging
- clean toilets
- swept chimneys
- no animals in streets
- the royal route strewn with petals and rushes.

The war with Spain rumbled on. Philip II hoped to use Ireland as a base to attack England, and sent two more Armadas in 1596 and 1597. Both were wrecked by storms, so he sent another 4,000 soldiers to support a rebellion led by Hugh O'Neill, earl of Tyrone. In 1598 O'Neill defeated an English army at the Battle of the Yellow Ford, then headed south, calling on other Irish lords to join him.

In 1599 Elizabeth sent her young favourite Robert Devereux, earl of Essex, to put down the rebellion. Essex, unhappy at being away from court, spent £300,000 in just five months without ever attacking O'Neill. In the end he agreed a truce and returned to court. The Queen was not impressed and stripped Essex of most of his titles. He was put under house arrest, charged with not carrying out orders. Angry at his treatment, in 1601 Essex made a half-hearted attempt to overthrow the government and soon found himself in the Tower. As a traitor, he couldn't be forgiven (in public, anyway), and he was executed on 25 February 1601. Elizabeth then dispatched her best general, Lord Mountjoy, who defeated the rebel army on Christmas Eve 1601.

Keeping up appearances

- The Queen knew all about public relations. Poets, playwrights, painters and songwriters were all paid to make her into a legend in her own lifetime. They called her names like Astraea (a goddess from Greek mythology) or Gloriana (from Edmund Spenser's famous poem about her, *The Faerie Queene*).

- Elizabeth I was like a Hollywood superstar and if she didn't like a portrait, it was destroyed. As she grew older, painters were given special 'face patterns' to make sure that their portraits made the Queen look younger. One rumour (probably not true) said she even banned mirrors so she wouldn't have to look at her crumbling face.

- If we can't trust any of the pictures, what did the ageing Queen Bess really look like? A German visitor described her black teeth, slightly hooked nose and wig of red hair. The Queen couldn't bear to have any of her rotten teeth removed, even though the bishop of London pulled one of his own teeth out in front of her to show how painless it was.

- To prove she was still up to the job, Elizabeth danced the galliard, an energetic leaping dance, every morning to keep herself fit. Even in her sixties, she could ride a distance of 10 miles (16 km).

By now Elizabeth was nearly 70. Though fit, she had lost her edge, and she increasingly relied on Robert Cecil to run the kingdom.[15] In March 1603 she retired to one of her favourite homes, Richmond Palace. Though growing weaker by the day, she stubbornly refused to lie down, instead choosing to stand for hours on end. When her death finally came on 24 March 1603 it was said that she passed away 'mildly like a lamb, easily like a ripe apple from the tree'.

She had not named a successor, so the throne passed to Scottish king James VI, who became James I of England. One of her ladies-in-waiting took off her sapphire ring and dropped it out of the window to Sir Richard Carey, who carried it north to James as proof of the queen's death. The journey took him less than 60 hours, a record that was only beaten by a team of coach and horses in 1832. With Elizabeth's death, the Tudor dynasty had ended, 118 years after it had begun at the Battle of Bosworth Field.[16]

15. She was also paranoid about the threat of assassination.
16. The Tudors who survive today are all descended from Henry VII's two daughters, Mary, Queen of France and Margaret, Queen of Scots. Elizabeth II is a direct descendent of Margaret in the 15th generation.

Speak like a Tudor

To give you a flavour of the times, get your tongue around some common Tudor words:

A is for **Apothecary** – a pharmacist
B is for **Bodkin** – a dagger, or a long pin for fastening clothing or pinning up hair
C is for **Cockshut time** – twilight
D is for **Duckies** – breasts (used by Henry VIII in a love letter to Anne Boleyn)
E is for **Eftsoons** – repeatedly or immediately
F is for **Fopdoodle** – an idiot
G is for **Gorebelly** – a paunch
H is for **Hochepot** – a mixture or stew, giving us the word 'hodgepodge'
I is for **Ire** – anger
K is for **Kim-kam** – crooked or strange
L is for **Leech** – a doctor or healer
M is for **Mead** – an alcoholic drink made from honey
N is for **Neaf** – a fist
O is for **Oratory** – a chapel
P is for **Privy** – a toilet
Q is for **Quat** – a pimple
R is for **Revelry** – fun and games
S is for **Sorely** – very
T is for **Trencher** – a plate made of stale bread
U is for **Usury** – moneylending
W is for **Wench** – a girl
X is for **eXhale** – draw your sword!
Y is for **Yeoman** – a servant who was born free
Z is for **Zounds** – good heavens!

Note: The Tudor alphabet only contained 24 letters; 'i' and 'j' counted as one letter, as did 'u' and 'v'.

Love like a Tudor

This poem attributed to Elizabeth I tells a sad story: she desperately loves someone but because she is queen, she has to hide her feelings. Some believe it was written about Francis, duke of Alençon, whom the Queen nicknamed her 'Little Frog'. Others argue that the poem was written with Robert Dudley in mind (pet name 'Sweet Robin').

I grieve and dare not show my discontent,
I love and yet am forced to seem to hate,
I do, yet dare not say I ever meant,
I seem stark mute but inwardly do prate.
I am and not, I freeze and yet am burned,
Since from myself another self I turned.

My care is like my shadow in the sun,
Follows me flying, flies when I pursue it,
Stands and lies by me, doth what I have done.
His too familiar care doth make me rue it.
No means I find to rid him from my breast,
Till by the end of things it be supprest.

Some gentler passion slide into my mind,
For I am soft and made of melting snow;
Or be more cruel, love, and so be kind.
Let me or float or sink, be high or low.
Or let me live with some more sweet content,
Or die and so forget what love ere meant.

feel like a Tudor

Visit these sites to soak up some Tudor atmosphere!

- **Tower of London.** Where Anne Boleyn, Lady Jane Grey and countless others got the chop. Worth a visit just to see the famous Traitors' Gate where prisoners were brought in by boat at high tide. The Tower also has an amazing collection of armour, including suits belonging to Henry VIII.

- **Hampton Court Palace, London.** Henry VIII loved Hampton Court so much that he 'persuaded' Cardinal Wolsey to give it to him. The King then rebuilt it into one of Europe's finest palaces. Hopefully you won't bump into the screaming ghost of Catherine Howard which is said to haunt the palace.

- **Hever Castle, Kent.** This spectacular castle was Anne Boleyn's childhood home. It contains a chilling collection of beheading swords and torture instruments as well as one of the best collections of Tudor portraits in England.

- **Longleat House, Warminster, Wiltshire.** One of the finest Elizabethan houses in the country. The great hall has changed little since the Virgin Queen's visit in 1574.

- **Shakespeare's Globe Theatre, London.** This remarkable reconstruction, close to the original site, gives a real flavour of open-air theatre in Elizabethan times.

- **Leeds Castle, Kent.** Henry VIII spent a fortune turning this into a luxury home, adding a whole new floor for Catherine of Aragon. But he may only have spent a few days here on his way to meet Francis I at the Field of the Cloth of Gold.

- **Westminster Abbey.** The burial place of Elizabeth I and Mary I; Mary, Queen of Scots; Anne of Cleves; Henry VII and his queen, Elizabeth of York.

- **Greenwich Palace.** Henry VIII was born here in 1491 and this palace remained one of his favourites. Though the original building was destroyed in the 17th century, the surrounding park is much as it was.

- **Eltham Palace, Greenwich.** Where Henry VIII spent his childhood. Again most of the Tudor palace is gone, with the exception of the magnificent great hall.

- **Knole Palace, Kent.** Given by Elizabeth I to the Sackville family in 1566, this grand house is stuffed with Tudor furniture and portraits.

- **Hatfield House.** Elizabeth I spent most of her childhood here and, though most of the old palace was demolished in the 17th century, the great hall where Elizabeth held her first Council of State still survives. You can also see famous portraits of Elizabeth, and her hat, gloves and stockings.

- **Windsor Castle.** One of Elizabeth I's main homes. The chapel was finished during Henry VIII's reign and Elizabeth also added many new buildings. It contains the famous painting of Henry VIII and his children Edward, Mary and Elizabeth, and a giant suit of armour built for Henry when he was 50.

- **Portsmouth.** One of Henry's favourite ships, the *Mary Rose*, sank off the Isle of Wight in 1545 but was salvaged in 1982. The wreck is preserved along with weapons, sailing equipment, naval supplies and all sorts of other objects used by the crew, providing a fascinating glimpse into Tudor life. In 2009 work began on a new purpose-built museum.

- **Ightham Mote, Kent.** This spectacular moated manor house is one of the most complete medieval or Tudor buildings in England. Highlights include the great hall, the crypt, and a Tudor chapel with a hand-painted ceiling.

- **National Portrait Gallery, London.** Home to many famous portraits of the Tudors – but remember, the painters were under strict instructions to make their subjects look as good as possible.

Act *like* a Tudor

The Tudors were made for the movies. Over the years, many famous actors have brought these big personalities to life on big and small screens, with very different results:

Henry VIII

- **The Private Life of Henry VIII (1936).** Actor Charles Laughton shows the vulnerable side of Henry – a lonely man at the mercy of his six wives (but didn't he execute two of them?).

- **Anne of a Thousand Days (1969).** Richard Burton's Henry is handsome, charismatic and ruthless. He delivers the classic line: 'Divorce is like killing – after the first time, it's easy.'

- **A Man For All Seasons (1966).** The King Henry played by Robert Shaw is everyone's nightmare boss: laughing and joking one minute, screaming with rage the next.

- **Carry on Henry (1971).** Forget the history as Sid James's Henry fails miserably to bump off his made-up queen, Marie of Normandy. Elizabethan audiences would probably have loved the bad jokes and dirty humour.

- **Henry VIII (2003).** Ray Winstone plays Henry as if he were a murdering gangster – which he probably was! To play the young, fit

Henry, Winstone had to diet for weeks. As Henry got older, he put on a fat suit!

- **The Tudors (2007).** Jonathan Rhys Meyers shows what a handsome devil the young Hal was. Unlike Winstone, he refused to put on weight or don a fat suit to play the ageing tyrant.

Elizabeth I

- **The Loves of Queen Elizabeth (1911).** The great French actress Sarah Bernhardt played Elizabeth I in this silent movie, which looks at her relationship with the earl of Essex.

- **Fire Over England (1937)** and **The Sea Hawk (1940).** Flora Robson shows two sides to Elizabeth in these swashbuckling adventures: sharp-tongued and dominating at court, kind and gentle in private.

- **The Private Lives of Elizabeth and Essex (1939)** starred the powerful actress Bette Davis as the Virgin Queen. To play the part, Davis had her eyebrows removed. She later complained they never grew back properly.

- **Elizabeth R (1971).** This TV series gives a very accurate version of Elizabeth's life, brilliantly played by Glenda Jackson. The actress even learned to play the virginals (an Elizabethan keyboard instrument) for the part. Some of the costumes were so heavy she couldn't stand up in them.

- **Blackadder, Part II (1985).** In this comedy, Miranda Richardson plays Elizabeth as the completely loopy 'Queenie'. Lots of fun!

- **Elizabeth (1998)** and **Elizabeth: The Golden Age (2007).** Though beautiful to look at, these movies play fast and loose with history. But Cate Blanchett does a wonderful job of showing how the young queen turned into a proud and ruthless monarch.

Others

- **The Execution of Mary Stuart (1895).** This silent film was made by Thomas Edison, the famous US inventor. Just one minute long, it was one of the first films ever made. Mary is played by a man, Robert Thomae.

- **The Prince and the Pauper (1937).** A film version of Mark Twain's novel in which Edward VI trades places with a poor boy from the streets who looks just like him. Twins Billy and Robert J. Mauch played the two boys.

- **Mary, Queen of Scots (1971).** Mary, Queen of Scots, played by Vanessa Redgrave, clashes with Elizabeth I, again played by Glenda Jackson. Though the two queens never met in real life, this is great drama!

- **Lady Jane (1986).** Helena Bonham Carter stars as the tragic Lady Jane Grey. Though the actress has dark eyes and hair, in reality Lady Jane had blond hair and brown eyes.

Sing like a Tudor

Legend has it this famous tune was written by Henry VIII for his lover Anne Boleyn. It's a nice idea but unlikely to be true. The words were first published in 1580 and the tune was described as 'new' in 1584.

A- las, my love, ye do me wrong, To cast me off dis- cour-teous-ly; And I have lo- ved you so long, De--ligh- ting in your com- pa- ny.

Green- sleeves was all my joy,

Green- sleeves was my de- light;

Green-sleeves was my heart of gold, And

who but la- dy Green-sleeves.

Eat like a Tudor

Tudor recipes were very vague – there was no list of ingredients, no amounts, and no cooking temperatures and times. Here is an original recipe for gilded marchpane, along with a modern version. This marzipan cake – made either as a disc or as a 3-D sculpture – was the centrepiece of a Tudor banquet. It was iced and, on special occasions, covered with a layer of gold. You can get something of the effect by using gold food colouring.

Original recipe

Take blancht[1] Almonds and sugar and beat them up into a Past,[2] and when you have beaten it into a Past, rowl[3] it out about the thickness that you will have your Marchpane Cakes to be and cut them in 3 square[4] pieces and set an Edge to them of the same past, and Impress[5] the Edges of them, then take Rose Watter and beat searced[6] sugar in it till it be as thick as Pancakes, butter and wet them within it and strew[7] a few of Bisketts in them and set them upon Wafers, and set them againe upon Papers and bake them, and keep them for your use.

1. blancht: blanched (cooked briefly in boiling water)
2. Past: paste
3. rowl: roll
4. 3 square: triangular
5. Impress: flatten
6. searced: sieved
7. strew: scatter.

Modern version (contains nuts)

Ingredients:
- 1 lb (450 g) ground almonds
- ½ lb (225 g) caster sugar
- 3 tablespoons (45 ml) rose-water

For the glaze:
- 1 tablespoon (15 ml) rose-water
- 3 tablespoons (45 ml) icing sugar

Method:

1 Preheat the oven to 150°C (300°F).

2 Mix the almonds, sugar and rose-water into a stiff paste. Knead until smooth. Put aside some of this marzipan for decoration and place the rest on a sheet of greaseproof paper.

3 Using a rolling pin, roll it into a disc about 1 cm thick. Smooth the edges with the back of a knife.

4 Bake for 15 mins then allow to cool for another 15 mins until firm.

5 To make the glaze, mix the rose-water and icing sugar in a small bowl. Paint this over the marzipan disc with a pastry brush. Place back in the oven and cook for another 5 mins.

6 Now for the creative bit. Roll out the remaining marzipan then cut into shapes or letters with pastry cutters. Paint these with edible gold or other food colouring. After taking the marzipan disc out of the oven, use these shapes to decorate it. Enjoy!

Glossary

alchemist A scientist who tried to turn cheap metals like lead and copper into gold. (It's impossible!)

ambassador The top diplomat who represents his or her country abroad.

apothecary A maker and seller of medicines.

armada A large fleet.

astrologer Someone who tries to predict the future from the positions of the Sun, Moon and planets.

bear-baiting A blood sport in which bears were tied to a post and attacked by a pack of dogs.

chronicle A history of events day by day or year by year.

civil war A war between rivals in the same country.

cockpit A place used for the blood sport of cock fighting.

codpiece A flap or pouch covering the front of the crotch of men's breeches.

consumption Another name for tuberculosis (or TB), a deadly disease which attacks the lungs.

coronation The crowning of a new king or queen.

courtier Someone who attends the court of a king, queen or other powerful person.

dowry A gift made by a bride's family to her bridegroom.

dynasty A line of royals or other leaders belonging to the same family.

excommunicate To banish someone from the Church. In Tudor times, this meant being sent to hell.

exiled Forced to leave your city or country, often as a punishment.

fool A jester.

headsman An executioner.

heir A person who expects to inherit a relative's property or titles.

heretic A person who holds religious beliefs which the Church does not approve of.

Huguenots French Protestants, many of whom were forced to leave France in the 16th and 17th centuries.

lady-in-waiting A noblewoman who attends a queen or princess (a sort of very high-class servant).

litter A chair or bed carried on two poles by footmen.

medieval Belonging to the Middle Ages, a period from about 450 to 1450 AD.

mercenary A professional soldier who fights for money, not out of loyalty to a ruler.

minstrel A professional musician or entertainer.

New World North and South America.

Parliament The English (later British) government, or the building where it meets.

pilgrimage A long journey to worship at a holy place.

plague A fast-spreading and often deadly disease.

Plantagenets The family name of a dynasty of English kings that reigned from 1154 to 1485.

privy A simple toilet, usually a bench with a hole in it, above a pit.

progress A royal tour around the country.

rapier A light, slender sword with a sharp point.

refugee A person forced to leave home for their own safety, often to another country.

treachery The act of betraying someone, especially a king or queen.

tyrant A harsh and cruel ruler.

ulcer An open sore or wound, often full of pus.

viol A stringed instrument, played with a bow.

Timeline of Tudor history

1485 Battle of Bosworth Field. Henry Tudor defeats and kills Richard III and is crowned as Henry VII.

1486–1487 Revolt of Lambert Simnel.

1491 Birth of Henry VIII.

1492 Henry VII's expedition to Boulogne in France. Signs Treaty of Etaples with Charles VIII of France.

1495–1497 Revolt of Perkin Warbeck.

1497 John Cabot reaches Newfoundland, Canada, and claims it for Henry VII.

1499–1500 Deadly plague kills 30,000 in London.

1501 Henry VII's son Arthur marries Catherine of Aragon.

1502 Prince Arthur dies.

1503 Henry VII's wife, Elizabeth of York, dies.

1509 Henry VII dies. Henry VIII becomes king and marries Catherine of Aragon.

1512 Wolsey becomes Henry VIII's chief minister.

1513 Henry VIII invades France. James IV of Scotland defeated at Battle of Flodden Field.

1516 Birth of Henry VIII's daughter, Mary I.

1517–1518 Outbreak of sweating sickness.

1520 Henry VIII meets Francis I of France at the Field of the Cloth of Gold.

1521 Duke of Buckingham executed. Secret treaty between Henry VIII and Emperor Charles V to invade France.

1526 Henry VIII starts chasing Anne Boleyn.

1527 Henry VIII asks Pope for divorce from Catherine of Aragon.

1530 Death of Wolsey.

1531 Catherine of Aragon banished from court.

1531–1535 England breaks with Catholic Church in Rome. Henry VIII becomes head of Protestant Church of England.

1533 Henry VIII marries Anne Boleyn in secret and is excommunicated by Pope Clement VII. Elizabeth I born. Thomas Cromwell becomes Henry VIII's chief minister. Thomas Cranmer becomes archbishop of Canterbury.

1535 Henry VIII first grows a beard. Anne Boleyn is beheaded. Henry VIII marries Jane Seymour. Thomas More is executed.

1536 Henry VIII badly injured in a jousting accident.

1536–1539 Henry VIII loots and destroys many of England's monasteries and churches.

1536–1537 Revolt known as Pilgrimage of Grace breaks out in northern England. Mary I agrees to renounce the throne. Leader of Pilgrimage of Grace, Robert Aske, hanged in York.

1537 Birth of Edward VI. Jane Seymour dies. Henry VIII authorises first English Bible.

1540 Henry VIII marries and divorces Anne of Cleves, then marries Catherine Howard.

1542 Catherine Howard beheaded. Henry VIII declared King of Ireland. Mary, Queen of Scots born.

1543 Henry VIII marries Catherine Parr. 9-month-old Mary, Queen of Scots is crowned. Mary I and Elizabeth I made heirs to the throne by Parliament.

1544 Henry VIII's forces capture Boulogne. Thomas Wriothesley becomes Lord Chancellor.

1545 *Mary Rose* sinks. English defeated by Scots at Battle of Ancrum Moor.

1547 Death of Henry VIII. Edward VI crowned king. Duke of Somerset becomes Lord Protector. Catherine Parr secretly marries Sir Thomas Seymour.

1547–1548 Sir Thomas Seymour tries to woo Elizabeth I. Catherine Parr dies.

1549 First *Book of Common Prayer*. Catholic revolts defeated in Devon, Cornwall and Norfolk. Duke of Northumberland overthrows duke of Somerset. Sir Thomas Seymour executed for planning to kidnap King Edward; Elizabeth I is linked to the plot.

1552 Duke of Somerset executed.

1553 Death of Edward VI. Revolt by duke of Northumberland and Lady Jane Grey defeated by Mary Tudor. She is crowned Mary I. Northumberland is executed.

1554 Protestant revolt led by Sir Thomas Wyatt is defeated by Mary I. Jane Grey is executed. Cardinal Pole reunites England with Catholic Church in Rome. Elizabeth I imprisoned in the tower for 8 weeks. Mary I marries Prince Philip of Spain.

1555 False news that Mary is pregnant. Elizabeth I becomes heir to Mary's throne.

1555–1558 280 Protestants burned on Mary's orders, including Cranmer.

1556 England declares war on France. Mary's husband Prince Philip becomes King Philip II of Spain.

1557 Anne of Cleves dies.

1558 English forces lose Calais to the French. Mary I dies. Elizabeth I is crowned. Sir William Cecil becomes her chief minister.

TIMELINE OF TUDOR HISTORY

1558–1563 Elizabeth ends religious strife in England by reforming Church of England.

1558–1559 Elizabeth makes peace with France.

1560 Sir Robert Dudley, the Queen's favourite, is suspected of murdering his wife.

1565 Mary, Queen of Scots marries Lord Darnley. Mary, Queen of Scots gives birth to James VI of Scots (later James I of England).

1567 Darnley murdered. Mary, Queen of Scots imprisoned and forced to abdicate her throne.

1569 Catholic rising in north defeated by Elizabeth I.

1570 Pope Pius V excommunicates Elizabeth I.

1572 Treaty of Blois between France and England.

1577–1581 Francis Drake sails around the world and is knighted on his return.

1584 Sir Walter Raleigh establishes a colony in North America, named Virginia after Elizabeth I.

1585 Elizabeth I sends English troops to help Protestant rebellion in Netherlands.

1586 Babington Plot against Elizabeth is defeated. Drake attacks Spanish fleet at Cádiz.

1587 Execution of Mary, Queen of Scots

1588 Defeat of the Spanish Armada.

1592–1602 Many of Shakespeare's plays first performed in south London.

1594–1603 Rebellion by Hugh O'Neill, earl of Tyrone, in Ireland.

1597 Earl of Essex fails to defeat O'Neill.

1601 Rebellion by Essex defeated; Essex executed.

1602 Spanish forces defeated at Kinsale in Ireland.

1603 Death of Elizabeth I. End of the Tudor dynasty. James I, the first Stuart king, comes to the throne.

Index

Very Peculiar Histories™

www.salariya.com
where books come to life!

The Salariya Book Company is a UK-based independent publisher of books for children which sells both domestically and internationally. Through our imprints Book House, Scribblers and Scribo we are dedicated to publishing books with real child appeal, using innovative concepts, high-quality illustrations, informative writing and, above all, humour to captivate the minds of young people. With a mind for the environment, all of our books are printed on paper from sustainable forests. Click the links below to visit our imprints' websites, read our Book House Blog or dive into a world of free interactive web books from the best-selling 'You Wouldn't Want To Be...' series.

The Salariya Book Company,
25, Marlborough Place,
Brighton,
East Sussex
BN1 1UB
England
United Kingdom

Tel: 01273 603306
Fax: 01273 621619

rights - srmc.murray@salariya.com
press - jamie.pitman@salariya.com
editorial - stephen.haynes@salariya.com
managing director - david@salariya.com

Follow us on Facebook and Twitter

Children's non-fiction and graphic novels

Fiction for children and teenagers

THE BOOK HOUSE BLOG
The Official Blog of The Salariya Book Company

The Book House blog competitions, giveaways and current news

Scribblers
Bright Start Right Start

www.youtube.com/user/BookHouse

Available on the App Store

FREE APP!

Download our free iPhone and iPad catalogue app. Go to http://bit.ly/c8zQuy or search for Salariya or Book House at the App Store

FREE WEB BOOK!

FREE WEB BOOKS!

Four free web books

TUDOR WARSHIP
TO BE RAISED

Plans are now well underway to raise the remains of the Tudor warship Mary Rose from the bed of the Solent off Portsmouth. A specially designed lifting cradle has been constructed and, weather permitting, it is hoped that the operation can be completed by October 1982.

The Mary Rose was launched at Portsmouth in July 1511. She was a carrack – an ocean-going vessel with tall 'castles' at bow and stern. She was 'made new' in 1536, and this may have involved fitting new gunports close to the waterline.

On 19 July 1545 the Mary Rose suddenly sank at the entrance to Portsmouth harbour while sailing out to attack a French fleet. She may have filled with water through her open gunports while trying to turn quickly. Most of her crew drowned – many were unable to escape because of the netting that was stretched across the upper deck to prevent enemies from boarding the ship.

HE
H
OP
FOR

For too lon
taurant have bee
But now w
Roof is open for
Which mea
men can enjoy o
atmosphere.
your table